In the Great Maelstrom

IN THE GREAT MAELSTROM

CONSERVATIVES IN POST–CIVIL WAR SOUTH CAROLINA

CHARLES J. HOLDEN

University of South Carolina Press

Published in Columbia, South Carolina, by the
University of South Carolina Press

Manufactured in the United States of America

06 05 04 03 02   5 4 3 2 1

Library of Congress Cataloging-in-Publication Data

Holden, Charles J.
   In the great maelstrom : conservatives in Post–Civil War South Carolina / Charles J.
Holden.
      p. cm.
   Includes bibliographical references and index.
   ISBN 1-57003-476-1 (cloth : alk. paper)
   1. South Carolina—History—1865– 2. South Carolina—Intellectual life. 3. South
Carolina—Politics and government—1865–1950. 4. Conservatism—South Carolina—
History—19th century. 5. Conservatism—South Carolina—History—20th century.
6. Reconstruction—South Carolina. 7. Intellectuals—South Carolina —History—19th
century. 8. Intellectuals—South Carolina—History—20th century. I. Title.
   F274.H73 2002 975.7—dc21   2002008018

To Mary Ann and Edward Holden

Contents

Acknowledgments

I am grateful for the support and encouragement from many friends and colleagues at Penn State, the University of North Carolina at Greensboro, St. Mary's College of Maryland, and various points in between. Special thanks go to Christine Adams, Aileen Bailey, Douglas Billings, Sam Chambers, Tom Stevens, Beverly Lehman, Bob Calhoon, Bill Link, Robert Shelton, Denise Kohn, Melissa Kean, Bill and Mary Ann Blair, Eileen Gallagher, Adrienne Middlebrooks, Phil Rutherford, Bryan Grove, Steve Knox, Jim Giesen, and from the University of South Carolina Press, Alex Moore and Scott Burgess. At times it seems I hardly read a book or write a sentence without consulting my good friend, Peter S. Carmichael.

I also want to express my gratitude to my former professors at Penn State University: Gary W. Gallagher, Thavolia Glymph, Isabel Knight, James Rambeau, and especially my mentor Nan E. Woodruff. Professor Woodruff also made it possible to add Eugene Genovese as an outside reader.

Finally, it is a pleasure to say thank you to my family. It is a steady source of comfort knowing that the "folks back home" in Iowa are wondering how I am doing and checking in regularly. Thanks then go to Ann and Gary Kendell, Mary Jo and Roger Kluesner, Rosemary and David Hoyt, Michael and Susan Holden, the whole gang of nieces and nephews, the Burke family, Betts Whitnell, and Bill Brunner. I also want to pass along my special appreciation for one of my closest readers, my uncle Richard Brunner. Lastly, I am incredibly fortunate to have Edward and Mary Ann Holden as my parents. I am so grateful to them for so much. Thanks, Mom and Dad.

IN THE GREAT MAELSTROM

Introduction

Could the regimes of states and ruling classes be given a new legitimacy in the minds of democratically mobilized masses? Much of the history of our period consists of attempts to answer this question. The task was urgent, because the ancient mechanisms of social subordination were often clearly breaking down.

—Eric Hobsbawm, *The Age of Empire, 1875–1914*

In the early 1880s Frederick A. Porcher, president of the South Carolina Historical Society, approved the membership of a young college graduate, Theodore D. Jervey Jr. The society relished its list of prominent, old Charleston family names such as Pinckney, Middleton, and Rutledge. These families represented the core of South Carolina's aristocratic, conservative leadership. Jervey's and Porcher's shared association with the South Carolina Historical Society highlights the striking expanse of American history that South Carolina's post–Civil War conservatives covered. Porcher, born in 1809, claimed childhood memories of United States victories over the British during the War of 1812. He served in the General Assembly of South Carolina in the 1830s, and in the 1850s he wrote a series of articles that helped shape the state's defense of slavery. Theodore D. Jervey Jr., born in 1859, became a fixture in Progressive Era Charleston and state politics, published a pamphlet on the causes of World War I, and lived long enough to marvel at the dropping of atomic bombs on Japan that ended World War II.

The linking of these two locally known and respected members of the state's elite, a link that connects the United States' early national period to the end of World War II, demonstrates what most would already assume: that South Carolina, even following the collapse of the Confederacy, remained a conservative state. Yet most would also agree that through industrialization and urbanization and by showing signs of economic prosperity, South Carolina by 1945 had changed in dramatic ways from the battered state that limped out of the Civil War and through the postwar decades. How was it that a state which underwent significant changes during these years managed to retain its staunch conservatism? Self-proclaimed conservatives carried forward key conservative values from the Old South through the late 1800s and well into the 1900s. These traditional conservative values, in turn, helped steer South Carolina's leaders through "restoration," populism, segregation, industrialization, progressivism, World War I, and the Great Depression and New

Deal. First, as one would expect, postwar conservatives continued to believe in white supremacy. Second, they still detested democratic, majoritarian rule, believing instead in elite (meaning themselves) and local rule over all, including over poor whites, for whom they often showed little regard. Third, postwar conservatives carried forward the antebellum belief that history was a living force from which a society could not escape. Antebellum conservatives invoked the past as part of their justification for continued existence of slavery. Postwar conservatives similarly defended the reestablishment of elite rule as a reflection of a historically sanctioned fact of South Carolina society. Through their particular reading of the past, South Carolina's conservatives believed that history had destined them to remain on top of a hierarchical social order, whether slave or free.

Believing in hierarchy, however, did not lead these conservatives to envision the kind of organic society that antebellum writers and intellectuals evoked. The antebellum conservative ideology was, after all, rooted in the institution of slavery, from which mutual responsibilities along the entire chain of hierarchy sprang. It is hard to argue that postwar conservatives ever developed a social vision as sophisticated as that of their antebellum predecessors. Postwar conservatism was more skeletal, relying on a few core beliefs that held conservatives together. But holding on was enough, and perhaps because of its lean features, postwar conservatism endured through the decades.

Although core conservative beliefs survived the Civil War, South Carolina was not impervious to regional movements for change. South Carolina's elite more often than not shaped the forces for change toward their three key conservative values—in contrast to Alexis de Tocqueville's mid-nineteenth-century lament for the French ruling elite, who were also reeling from revolution.[1] Not all of the state's conservative spokesmen died with the Confederacy; nor could the conservative intellectual tradition have completely disappeared. W. J. Cash explained as much in 1941 by noting that the South "is a tree with many rings, with its limbs and trunk bent and twisted by all the winds of the years, but with its tap root in the Old South."[2]

One quick measure of the state's durability can be found in Katharine Du Pre Lumpkin's memoir, much of which is set in South Carolina. As Lumpkin described her dramatic "time of change" in 1945, when she concluded that segregation had to end, she noted specifically that she was attempting to break from the white South's racism and its suffocating reverence for the

past. Beliefs in white supremacy and the living power of the past are two of
the core values of postwar conservatism.[3]

The assumption that South Carolina remained conservative has kept scholars from even bothering to ask how South Carolina remained a philosophi-
cally conservative state. South Carolina's elite knew all too well by mid-1865
that the South would never be able to go back to its antebellum ideals completely. Members of the state's conservative leadership, however, did not
retreat into a bunker mentality after the war. Instead they continued wrestling
with what South Carolinian Leonidas Spratt in 1858 described as "society in
its secret movements."[4] Here the student of South Carolina can benefit from
an observation of the state's European conservative contemporaries by Arno
Mayer, who wrote, "There has been a marked tendency to neglect or under-
play, and to disvalue, the endurance of old forces and ideas and their cunning
genius for assimilating, delaying, neutralizing" the waves of change crashing
over the old regimes.[5]

A careful reading of the abundant speeches, pamphlets, and letters from
after the Civil War reveals that South Carolina's conservatives shared and
actively engaged in a line of questioning that could be paraphrased as "What
can we still believe in?" As it turned out, the answer was "Plenty." Speaking
at the College of Charleston's 1871 commencement, William D. Porter, former president of the South Carolina Senate and leader of the secessionist
1860 Association, explained simply: "Many things here are changed, but all is
not changed."[6] Historians have left comments such as these unexamined for
any evidence of an earnest philosophical adjustment to the Confederacy's
defeat. William Porter's straightforward observation, especially his insistence
that *all* was not changed, is crucial to understanding postwar conservatism.
It speaks to the constant tension among conservatives trying to weigh the
forces for change against their definition of social order, a tension that in
South Carolina's case did not end with military defeat.

Evidence abounds that in their search for answers the state's conservatives also understood clearly the influence they would still have over their fellow South Carolinians. Charlestonian Thomas M. Hanckel, writing in 1867,
acknowledged that while his fellow elite could not simply go on believing
entirely as they had before the war, there was no reason to despair. He congratulated them both for their "intelligent submission to necessity" *and* their
continued "regard for social order."[7] The South Carolina historian William J.
Rivers invoked the Old South and urged the state's elite to "infuse her nature"

into the new order.[8] Wade Hampton, the former Confederate general who later led the overthrow of Reconstruction in South Carolina, sounded a similar postwar message; mixing possibility with acceptance, he warned his fellow members of the elite, "If we cannot direct the wave it will overwhelm us."[9] Hampton's straightforward remark reveals that even *after* the defeat of the Confederate army, the destruction of the Confederate nation, and the end of slavery, the general still worried about the possibility of conservative South Carolinians such as himself being "overwhelmed."[10]

State political studies of South Carolina view the "restoration" in 1877 in terms of the traditional elite's effective use of noblesse oblige as a bare-knuckled strategy to divide and conquer the expanded, biracial democracy created by the state's 1868 constitution. William J. Cooper Jr. has summarized the conservative mission as an effort to establish a state "controlled by native whites" and bolstered by an educational system that "inculcated the values and ideals of the past."[11] Historian Walter Edgar has noted that those of the state's elite who gathered in September 1865 to write South Carolina's first postwar constitution intended fully to uphold the "tradition of letting the voters have as little say as possible about their government" and that again in 1876 conservatives sought "politically and socially" to "re-create as much as possible the world of antebellum South Carolina, a world in which they and their kind held sway."[12] It is evident that conservatives' effort to re-create as much of the Old South as possible was indistinguishable from their agenda to influence the state's politics. Mixed in with the tales of woe and the weepy memories of days gone by, the state's conservatives sent their fellow South Carolinians a message. While many of their lamentations on the present and nostalgia for the past strike the modern reader as being maudlin and sometimes even silly, they should not be ignored. In their obsession with their own past, South Carolina's conservatives promoted specific values from the Old South and an exclusive group of "native whites" to govern the state.

A southern perspective is nearly absent from people's understanding of American conservatism from 1865 to the 1930s.[13] Clinton Rossiter and Russell Kirk, two of the foremost scholars of American conservatism, both suggest that following the defeat of the Confederacy, the South "for a long time . . . [had] no philosophers," in Kirk's words.[14] Intellectual historians therefore too often turn their attention away from southern conservatives after 1860 and seldom pay a return visit until they deal with the beginning of Southern Agrarians' assault on the New Deal and industrialism. Left behind is an unexamined, murky image of postwar southern conservatism as it is refracted from several angles off the voluminous studies of the Lost Cause, the New South, southern populism, southern progressivism, the rise of Jim Crow, and on into the twentieth century. But to these South Carolinians, their conservatism came first and the issues were not as separate or isolated as historians often require them to be. Consider, for example, William Watts Ball, a conservative newspaper editor born in 1868. In the experience of this one man's lifetime, Ball considered *all* of the following, often overlapping, questions: Should the state promote industrial development or remain true to its economic foundation in agriculture? Should South Carolina voters in 1890 welcome populist leaders, Ben Tillman, or stay with the state's traditional rulers? To what extent should South Carolinians revere the Lost Cause versus accepting national reunification? Was racial segregation by law wise or even necessary? Should the South support American imperialism in Cuba or the Philippines? Should black southerners be allowed to fight in World War I? Should southern states adopt Prohibition, child labor laws, woman suffrage, compulsory education? What caused the Great Depression? Should a conservative, white southern Democrat vote for Franklin Roosevelt by the late 1930s? Should a white southern Democrat vote for Harry Truman or Strom Thurmond in 1948? For conservatives such as Ball, his belief in white supremacy, his relentless opposition to democracy, and his understanding of the state's past guided him through these bewildering questions of the post–Civil War decades.

M. E. Bradford is one of the few scholars who has considered southern conservatism through the postwar decades and into the twentieth century. In *Remembering Who We Are: Observations of a Southern Conservative*, Bradford relied on Frank Owsley's *Plain Folk in the Old South* to argue that antebellum southerners managed to create a society with ranks but with fluidity between the ranks. Planters wielded power but still considered the yeomen's pride, while yeomen could show deference to the planters while keeping their self-respect. It was, Bradford argued, not until the overthrow of Reconstruction that "representative spokesmen for the aristocracy turned their backs on the ancient alliance for a handful of Yankee silver." In the postbellum decades the "various crafts, roles, and stations" of the Old South had "ceased to be mutually supportive." Lamenting this fracturing of Old South society, Bradford spread the blame around: "After 1878, as a consequence of foreign *isms*, profitless compromises, and Yankee schoolmarms—to say nothing of . . . 'individualism' in high places—the social bond that had given unity to the white South became more and more attenuated." Here Bradford left the postbellum

South until he focused on the 1930s, as other scholars have done. Since 1932, he argued, the South, "though it has remained the nation's most conservative section, has nonetheless come closer and closer to a politics of class struggle."[15]

This study contends that the social bond between white South Carolinians was sorely challenged before and long after Reconstruction. A close look at their private and public thoughts reveals that South Carolina's traditional elite willingly, repeatedly, and without the lure of Yankee silver distanced themselves from their white brethren. While they believed in white supremacy, post–Civil War and post-Reconstruction conservatives' efforts in South Carolina were not by a wide margin solely a struggle to justify white domination over the black population. The conservatives in this study openly feared the politicization of poor whites and hoped that an elite-led regime would seize control over them as well. Life in a free-labor South Carolina severely and repeatedly tested the Old South beliefs in white supremacy and elite rule previously held together by slavery. To whatever extent antebellum South Carolina was a white democracy built on the foundation of slavery before the war, emancipation and the inclusion of African Americans in the political state upset the arrangement mightily.[16] Freedom and the constitutional changes that formally politicized the former slaves could not help but stir, with good reason, the deep insecurities of poorer whites. Meanwhile, the postwar elite in South Carolina observed warily that intense poverty and widespread illiteracy were not exclusive to African Americans.

This study's conclusions come close to those of George Brown Tindall's in *The Persistent Tradition in New South Politics*. Tindall found that a bedrock of conservatism supported the transition from "Bourbonism to progressivism," albeit at a price. Citing the observations of Albion Tourgée, Tindall noted that the Bourbon "defense of community had a way of becoming the defense of vested interest and class distinction, and vice versa. Such a connection was at work earlier in the secession movement, as it would be later in responses to populism and the New Deal." Postwar elites' "ultimate achievement," Tindall argued, was "the reconciliation of tradition with innovation." As two examples he cited the elite's comparatively moderate racial policies, signaling perhaps "a clue that class interest was more important . . . than racial dogma." The postwar elite innovated again, said Tindall, by "accepting another new truth, the Industrial Revolution." Skillfully, however, they moved to accept the New South while retaining the sense of hierarchy, deference, and sentimentality of the Old South.[17]

The argument that South Carolina's conservative tradition was severely challenged but responsive to the destruction of the slave society fits with the scholarship on other elite groups and their ability to withstand change. As the Italian sociologist Vilfredo Pareto once observed, the power of the elite can be characterized by its "slow and continuous transformation. It flows on like a river, never being today what it was yesterday." For South Carolina between 1860 and the 1940s this image fits reasonably well. A conservative slaveholding planter of 1860 may not have easily comprehended all the dynamics of a new upcountry mill town of 1914. But he surely would have empathized with the southern progressives' desire, as the self-defined "best" in society, to assert control over an "unruly" mill-hand class. The extent to which South Carolina's conservatives successfully instilled their values into the forces for change in their state again calls to mind Pareto's river metaphor depicting power relations over time. He noted that violent storms sometimes produce floods that disrupt and alter, usually only slightly, the flow of the river. But before long it "resumes its slow transformation. The flood has subsided, the river is again flowing normally in its wonted bed."[18]

Scholars of tradition have observed that the core values and lessons of a tradition are always being reevaluated through time by its followers.[19] Few people willingly cling to a system of belief knowing that its destination is oblivion. Put simply, these South Carolinians were not like Edmund Ruffin, the fiery Virginian who committed suicide at the end of the war rather than live in a free-labor South. Rather, these South Carolinians understood that, as Allen Tate would later describe it, "the tradition is there to work on"; Tate went on to say that the South was indeed the "home of a spirit" but added that "this mansion . . . was incidently made with hands."[20] Along the same lines, Jaroslav Pelikan noted in his work on the history of tradition its "all-too-human" source.[21] Elizabeth Fox-Genovese argued convincingly that with the defeat of slavery, history became a "source of anxiety" for southern conservatives and that the harshness of defeat and need for consolation contributed to a postwar literary "fantasy of ladies and cavaliers presiding over happy darkies amidst lush foliage and endlessly sunny skies."[22]

South Carolina writers have certainly created their share of fantasy history in the postwar decades. But for some conservatives, the past offered more than justification of the past or consolation in the present. Even with the revolution of emancipation, conservatives argued, society still needed tradition, and thankfully, they felt, South Carolina had one: governance from a local elite, racial harmony through racial hierarchy, and a particular reading of history that validated both. As Ben Robertson wrote in *Red Hills and Cotton,* "The past that Southerners are forever talking about is not a dead past—it is a chapter from the legend that our kinfolks have told us, it is a living past, living for a reason."[23] Even though Robertson went on to laud the virtues of the state's poor white population, few conservatives would have argued with his explanation of the role history should play. The state's conservatives would certainly have found agreement in William A. Percy's statement in *Lanterns on the Levee* that "in the South our anxiety is not to find new ideas, but to bring to realization old ones which have been tested and proved by years of anguish —a far more difficult undertaking."[24] Allen Tate, Ben Robertson, William Faulkner, and Margaret Mitchell were all part of the resurgence of southern writing in the 1920s and 1930s. Scholars of the southern renaissance point as a source of creativity to the engagement between these writers and southern history—that they represent a "recovering" of a tradition and history.[25] This study contends that the engagement with the past continued from 1865 to where the Tates and Faulkners of the South weighed in. Tradition, as George Brown Tindall observed of the postwar South, "has a stubborn way of asserting itself."[26]

Opting for depth over numbers, this study examines the writing of four individuals from conservative, established South Carolina families (although, as will be evident, not to the total exclusion of other figures). Since there is no shortage of primary source material for post–1865 southern conservatives, this approach may be likened to listening to four soloists standing in front of a small but full-throated choir. These four individuals offer opportunities to examine how conservatives wrestled to make sense of their world and how they conveyed that sense to others in different ways: as a college professor, as a politician, as a patrician scholar and fiction writer, and as a newspaperman.

Frederick A. Porcher was born into an old lowcountry family whose Huguenot ancestors came to South Carolina before the American Revolution. Among Porcher's grandfathers was a British Loyalist who had his land confiscated and later was amerced for his troubles.[27] By the time he received a professorship in history and belles lettres at the College of Charleston in 1848, Porcher's thinking reflected the emerging proslavery ideology. His writings cast a sharp eye on the changes being wrought from the industrializing British and northern societies. Porcher, like other proslavery intellectuals, maintained his belief that the slave South would be able to stay safely on the margins of the free-labor, capitalist world. His contribution to the proslavery critique lies in his insightful examination of the intellectual conformity generated by the emerging bourgeois ideology and the cult of progress. Together, he believed, they formed a powerful but dangerous "school of political economy" that "imperiously demands that by her standards alone shall be judged every act and every opinion of mankind."[28]

Porcher's postwar writings shed light on the initial conservative attempts to reshape old values within the dominant, free-labor, capitalist society. Like other postwar conservatives, Porcher quite logically concluded from four years of destruction and ultimate defeat that the forces generated from a capitalist economy were stronger than the South's ability to hold it at bay. Here Porcher exemplified Thomas Hanckel's praise for the conservatives' "intelligent submission to necessity." Once convinced, other conservative ideals fell back into place. He concluded that economic forces were natural forces that left human society surprisingly free to arrange itself according to other "natural" values such as intelligence and race. History, according to Porcher, was the surest guide to determine who in society possessed these superior qualities. To his postwar students at the College of Charleston, Porcher presented as self-evident through history that a stable society required white supremacy, limited democracy, and local rule by the traditional elite.

The public life of one of Porcher's antebellum students, Edward McCrady Jr., represents both the opportunities and dangers of carrying conservative principles of the Old South into the political tumult of postwar South Carolina. Born in 1833, McCrady was also of an old, prominent Charlestonian family. Edward McCrady Sr., his father, was a slave owner who gained wealth as one of the city's more successful antebellum lawyers. McCrady joined his father as an attorney in the 1850s and then joined the Confederate army in 1861, serving in the First Regiment of the South Carolina Volunteers under Gen. Maxcy Gregg. He saw considerable action early, was wounded both at Second Manassas and at Fredericksburg, and had the rank of lieutenant colonel at the end of the war. Following the war McCrady returned to Charleston to practice law. As did many of the elite of the late 1800s, McCrady enjoyed additional careers, in his case as a state politician and a renowned historian.

As a state congressman through the 1880s, McCrady gained local notoriety through his open advocacy of disfranchisement of illiterate white and black voters. He believed that the state's traditional ruling elite, now back in power, was charged with the duty to protect the vote by the state constitution of 1868. McCrady introduced legislation that established a literacy requirement for voting. Under McCrady's Eight-Box Law the voter needed to be able to read the names of the candidates and the offices in order to place the ballots in the corresponding boxes. An illiterate voter placing his vote for lieutenant governor in the box marked "governor," for instance, would be automatically disqualified. Proposal of his Eight-Box Bill in 1881 prompted an angry outcry from poorer, illiterate white voters. But McCrady explained to his fellow conservatives that as the traditional leaders of the state, "*we* must not shrink from the enforcement of the rule even on their account."[29] The Eight-Box Law passed in 1882, amended to allow election officials flexibility in offering assistance to (white) voters. Therefore McCrady's efforts never materialized as he hoped, and instead he helped spur an openly antiaristocratic reaction among white voters that culminated in the gubernatorial election of Ben Tillman in 1890.

McCrady's bold statements and political downfall taught the next generation of conservatives, including Theodore D. Jervey Jr., that conservatism needed new methods by which to spread its ideas and influence. As a son of the upcountry, Ben Robertson later wrote, "In Carolina from 1750 to 1860 we lost to Charleston; since that time Charleston has lost to us."[30] Conservatives such as those covered in this study would have had to concede, especially after 1890, that Robertson's formulation held more than a degree of truth. From a family whose Carolina roots dated back to 1740, Theodore Jervey Jr. was the son of a wealthy cotton and rice factor in Charleston. Jervey practiced law in the early 1880s and then flirted with reform as a pro-Tillman editorial writer for the short-lived *Charleston World*. Shortly after Tillman's election, Jervey became chairman of the Charleston Democratic Club, and in 1895 he was appointed city recorder for Charleston, a position he held until 1931. Firmly ensconced within the established Charleston political community, Jervey soon grew wary of "the people" and disgusted with the Tillman movement's pyrotechnics.

Theodore Jervey's writings, always adhering to the core conservative values of elite rule, white supremacy, and the power of history, also reflected the awareness that the conservative philosophy needed different strategies after the turn of the century. Jervey utilized fiction and the newly christened "scientific" techniques of historical research. His 1905 novel, *The Elder Brother,* was a lurid account of race relations during Reconstruction. Set in a fictional South Carolina, the novel applauded a society that recognized the need for racial hierarchy. But Jervey's novel also raised questions over the political chicanery and violence used to solidify white rule. Jervey's leading characters—members of the fictional state's elite—blamed the simplistic political solution of "white rule" on the poorer rural whites and worried over what the future held under such an arrangement. In an unpublished manuscript titled "Love Blinds?," set in the post-Reconstruction lowcountry, Jervey was even harder on the local poor whites. His aristocratic characters regarded their poor white neighbors as being as hopeless as their black neighbors.

In his 1925 book *The Slave Trade: Slavery and Color,* Jervey again argued that state laws disfranchising and segregating blacks were contrived solutions that ignored, as Jervey saw it, the strain on the white population caused by the mere presence of a black majority. Jervey insisted that the "diffusion" of the state's African American population throughout the rest of the nation would produce salutary results. Along the way he cited census data and lauded British imperialist policy (by which elite colonial administrators governed multiracial colonies) to demonstrate how traditional conservative beliefs in white supremacy and rule by the intelligent "best" could finally reign in a South Carolina with a white majority.

The worldview of William Watts Ball carries this study through to the atomic age and the stirring of the civil rights movement in the 1940s. Ball's father, Beaufort Ball, had been a prominent slaveholder, a Confederate veteran, and later one of Wade Hampton's chief lieutenants in the 1876 campaign to end Reconstruction. In the 1890s William Watts Ball began to write for the state's largest newspapers and eventually served as editor for Columbia's *The State* and later the *Charleston News and Courier.*

Ball's writing shows the conservative response to yet another wave of change. The forces for change unleashed by World War I threatened the southern elite social world rooted by then in segregation and disfranchisement. Woodrow Wilson proclaimed that the war would make the world safe for democracy, and war mobilization drew black South Carolinians into the military. From a southern conservative's perspective, this was a nightmare: African American soldiers trained by the federal government to fight for more democracy. Linking himself to European conservatives staving off revolution in the post–World War I years, Ball confided to his diary, "How can one live in South Carolina and not be Tory or Junker? 'Democracy?' 'Pure Democracy?' Have we not the 'Afro-American' with us?"[31] The traditional conservative values of white supremacy and elite rule (and with that a disdain for democracies) were alive and well in Ball's thoughts. Through the editorial columns of *The State* and the *News and Courier,* through pamphlets, and through a book, *The State That Forgot: South Carolina's Surrender to Democracy,* Ball poured forth his convictions that mass democracy at home had weakened the body politic while economic and political centralization at the national level threatened local elite rule and white southern political superiority.

In February 1933 William Watts Ball wrote to a friend outlining his already fierce resistance to the impending Franklin Roosevelt administration. Citing his own childhood memories of the Wade Hampton campaign to end Reconstruction, Ball noted, "I am an old-timer brought up in a conservative school."[32] From Frederick Porcher and Edward McCrady, whose lives spanned the transition from a slave to a free society, to Theodore Jervey and William Watts Ball, who witnessed the rise of South Carolina's industrial age as well as the world's nuclear age, the old "conservative school" remained open in South Carolina. The conservative school underwent renovation from time to time, but crucial parts of the original structure remained intact from 1860 to the 1940s.

CHAPTER ONE

The Evil of This Philosophy

Frederick Porcher and the Southern Critique of Progress, 1831–1860

On 4 July 1831 in Pineville, South Carolina, despite being "excessively frightened" by public speaking, Frederick A. Porcher proclaimed the end to the
long story of mankind as "one of gloom and darkness."[1] Porcher felt certain
that the United States represented the final triumph over "ignorance, with all
its train of concomitant evils, prejudice, superstition, bigotry, and tyranny,
[which] had always held undisputed sway over both the minds and bodies of
men."[2] The speech at Pineville, a village of summer residence for lowcountry
planter families, revealed a young southern mind inspired by the political and
intellectual revolutions sweeping the European-American world. Porcher
infused the early portion of his oration with republican sensibilities on the
irreversible march of progress driven by the power of individual, rational
thought over time. Yet before concluding his speech, Porcher, fresh out of
Yale College and still a young plantation owner, began to take note of disturbing trends in American society. Porcher was just beginning to sense the
formidable challenge that the rise of bourgeois liberalism and its attendant
faith in democracy presented to southern conservatives. His development
by the 1850s into a harsh and perceptive critic of bourgeois liberalism and
democracy highlights an intellectual movement that coalesced in a distinctive
Old South conservatism as tensions between the free and slave societies grew.
Within this tense environment Porcher worked his thoughts into convictions
that would stay with him his remaining days: beliefs in white supremacy, in
elite rule over the majority, and in the present power of the past. But on 4
July 1831 all that lay in the future, and Porcher relished the moment. He
wrote later of his address, "I got over all diffidence and acquitted myself
well."[3] Afterward he accepted the hearty congratulations from his fellow
planters and picnickers and then met Rebecca Branford Rhodes, who would
become his first wife—in all, a good day.

Frederick A. Porcher was born at Cedar Springs, the plantation of his
father, George Porcher, in Saint John's Berkeley in 1809. The Porchers were
a large, wealthy, lowcountry family whose connections through marriage
and relations included such prominent Carolina names as DuBose, Palmer,

Ravenel, and Mazyck. Like many planters, Frederick Porcher developed an interest in politics, literature, and history. He counted among his friends and acquaintances such notable South Carolina figures as William Gilmore Simms, James Henry Hammond, Christopher G. Memminger, William Henry Trescot, and James Petigru. He was elected to the South Carolina House of Representatives in 1832, 1836, and 1838 and finally received an appointment to teach at the College of Charleston in 1848, where he remained until his death in 1888. His contributions to the *Southern Quarterly Review* and *Russell's Magazine,* in addition to his College of Charleston lectures, provide an instructive look into the mind of a southern intellectual who read widely and wrote thoughtfully on history, representative government, and political economy.[4]

In his 1831 address (delivered on the day when Nat Turner's rebellion was to have taken place) Porcher credited Martin Luther and Galileo as having first pierced the "darkness" of history as the product of ignorance, superstition, and tyranny. He singled out Luther specifically for his impact on the American experience, and claimed that the Protestant Reformation released "the mind" to undertake "the bold and novel attempt of thinking for itself." Led by the intellectual descendants of Luther, the American independence movement was a new and unique chapter in human history. The birth of the United States marked "the effect of the march of the intellect as well as the cause of the further progress of the mind towards perfection." In this new American chapter of human history, "the forms and ceremonies of the old world were useless and cumbrous." As a people moving toward revolution, the American colonists had to "accustom the mind to reject the old prejudices and attachments." Distance and time freed colonial Americans from their burdensome past until, "having perceived the inutility of that which was once deemed indispensable, the mind was led gradually to inquire without horror into the expediency of rejecting the whole system."[5]

For Porcher, the successful drive for independence validated the intellectual revolution, liberating the American mind further from superstition and the new American citizen from history. The American mind "acquired a new impulse, and seemed to delight in forgetting all traces of the past." America's glory, as Porcher presented it in 1831, rested squarely on the rational individual who both generated and prospered from the transforming powers of American society. "He would be rash indeed," Porcher continued, "who would venture to impose a limit to their progress." This was, he believed, "the dawn of a day which shall have no end," and the advance of time would be "followed by a corresponding progress of the human mind." The darkness of history with which he began his speech was "to us forever past." The model of the American experience would, Porcher proclaimed, "quickly dispel the mists which hover over less enlightened nations. There can be no resisting the truth of this proposition." Speaking during the full rush of Jacksonian politics, however, Porcher also voiced fears of partisan politics, an excessive interest in making money, and a potentially untenable relationship between the South and the federal government. "Pecuniary" obsessions threatened to undermine Americans' love of liberty, while "violent party animosity" spread its divisive influence. These factors were worrisome but still no cause for alarm. Reason would sustain national progress: "With reason for our guide, and truth for our lamp, we shall stand unhurt amid the shock of revolutions."[6]

The looming nullification crisis provided many South Carolinians with the ideas and language of separation from the union. Porcher hinted along these same lines for his fellow planters. He noted that while Americans' love of liberty was indeed strong, should *their* liberty ever become endangered, reasonable persons would have to rebel, lest "an overweening attachment to the institutions founded by our ancestors, should cause us to forget our duty to ourselves." In 1831 reason was still the key for Porcher. He presented his case for a future southern independence within the same framework of rationalism he established for American independence. "Free and reflecting men" could yet safeguard their principles by dissolving the union and standing apart from the "imperfect and ambitious man, with his mania for legislation." Porcher asked, "Is that a cause why the friends of rational liberty should repine?" Certainly not, he answered. A stronger tie than "parchment" held rational men together. That tie was "the sacred spirit of liberty," and Porcher assured his listeners that "her dwelling is not necessarily with political confederacies—her confidence is not in written constitutions."[7]

With his skepticism of written constitutions, his concerns over the money-making zeal exhibited by his countrymen, and his fears that tawdry partisanship accompanied Jacksonian democracy, Porcher showed clear signs of the conservatism to come in the 1850s. In fact, Porcher's conservative principles emerge strongly enough that the early portion of the address could be viewed as the idealism of a well-schooled, young college graduate. What was significantly different about Porcher's essays in the 1850s was his recognition that even reason, of which he spoke so confidently in 1831, was no longer just an admirable quality possessed by the enlightened individual. Reason and its kin, progress, had been transformed into weapons now held in the arsenal of an aggressive northern society. In these later articles Porcher also taught his readers how ideas and language have real political and economic impact. But would he and other southern intellectuals be able to find or appropriate the right words and ideas to defend the South's slave-based society against the onslaught of liberal ideology and language?

In the years between the 4 July 1831 speech and his return to public writing in the late 1840s and 1850s, Porcher reexamined his views on progress, history, and governance. From his home plantation Somerton, Porcher was elected the captain of the local militia, a position he described as "a sort of chief of Police in the parish." He became the secretary for the local antitariff association and was reelected to the General Assembly of South Carolina three times during the 1830s, including once as a nullifier in 1832. Porcher made the planter's obligatory tour of Europe, visiting England, Scotland, France, Italy, and Belgium. These were, however, also difficult years. Both his first wife, Rebecca Rhodes, and his second wife, Emma Gough, died before the 1850s.[8]

Porcher spent the 1830s and 1840s as a full-time planter, at one point owning over one hundred slaves. But these were difficult years for nearly all South Carolina planters.[9] South Carolinians blamed their economic hardship on a high protective tariff that discouraged the introduction of foreign money into the American economy by inflating the prices of northern manufactured items. Decreased foreign purchases, low cotton prices, and acres of worn-out land drove thousands of South Carolinians west to Alabama and Mississippi to put newer land into production. The persistent financial insecurity of the planter's life forced a change in Porcher's life as well.[10] He sought and obtained a professorship at the College of Charleston in 1848.

As Drew Gilpin Faust has noted, careers for intellectuals in the Old South were few and unrewarding.[11] Porcher used his connections to secure a professorship of belles lettres and history.[12] Porcher did not, however, share the sense of alienation central to the lives and intellectual efforts of the members of Faust's "sacred circle." Secure with his place in the lowcountry intellectual community, he had no need to argue himself into relevance. By the time his writings appeared in public once again, Porcher's outlook fit squarely within the emerging southern conservative worldview.[13]

An aggressive northern abolition movement fueled rising sectional tension in the 1840s and 1850s and prompted a passionate, complex defense of slavery by southern intellectuals. Porcher's acquaintances James Henry Hammond and William Gilmore Simms were among the leading architects of a conservative perspective depicting slavery as a reflection of natural hierarchies sanctioned by God and history. They argued that plantation hierarchies of whites over blacks, masters over slaves, and men over women more closely resembled nature's or God's plan than did the abstract equality of individuals in free-labor ideology. The plantation household and economy offered natural sources of stability against the chaotic industrial societies of the North and England.[14] Proslavery southern intellectuals such as Frederick Porcher defended their slave society and in doing so also trained their well-schooled eyes on the weaknesses within free societies.

Porcher's argument that bourgeois liberalism generated a destructively narrow, if powerful, way of thinking contributed a penetrating analysis of modern thought to the growing southern conservative critique of free-labor ideology. Once he had observed that liberalism's utilitarian logic had worked its way into literature, religion, and one's understanding of history, Porcher abandoned his 1831 argument that the power of individual, rational thought always led to moral and material progress. Porcher now discovered that the world was "two-fold in nature. As light and darkness alternately sway the physical universe, so the moral world has its front and obverse."[15] Error, evil, and weakness were all still alive and well, he concluded, and would forever accompany the constantly changing human experience.

Porcher's new views on the nature of progress and the moral world forced him to reassess his understanding of the past. The results of this rethinking placed him well outside the buoyant, nationalistic, Manifest Destiny outlook shared by many Americans at midcentury. Porcher now challenged both the modern historical consciousness (and the lack of it) and its purveyors. Attacking along a wide front, Porcher argued that the romanticized, nationalist historical thought was too narrow, too individualistic, and not appreciative of the complexities that the past brings to the present. He wrote that, looking at the distant past, "we make ourselves the central point from which everything is to be regarded, by which everything is to be judged. . . . We . . . complacently pronounce as dark the age which preceded the discovery of America, and contemptuously affect to pity those who lived before the flood of light which is characteristic of modern civilization."[16] Porcher saw the focus on the American self as the "central point" of all history as part of the dangerously simplifying tendencies within liberal thought encouraging the fallacy that people could break cleanly from the past and that the human experience was getting better on all counts.

As he had in 1831, Porcher still cited the Protestant Reformation as the seminal event in the life of the modern mind. The Protestant intellectual revolution, he noted, also sparked the creation of historical interpretations tracking human progress that were, understandably, "rigourously protestant." But from this modern, "protestant" viewpoint, he claimed, "we lose some of the noblest lessons of the middle ages, and are led to prejudicial views of the only men who gave to those ages character and nobility."[17] Pointedly, Porcher, an Episcopalian, found among the noble lessons from the Middle Ages the value of a stable, authoritarian, and far-from-republican institution—the Catholic Church—during the subsequent centuries of social and political unrest.

It is clear that in his critique of Protestant history the intensifying sectional crisis of the late antebellum years was never far from his mind. In Porcher's reading of the eleventh-century Catholic Church and its confrontational, authoritarian Pope Gregory VII are to be found characteristics similar to those that southern conservatives lauded in a Christian slave society and in a good southern planter. Chiding the dominant Protestant interpretation of Gregory VII as one "in which appears no redeeming quality," Porcher stressed the context of eleventh-century Europe, in whose "chaotic state the church alone afforded any hope of security."[18]

Not only did Porcher depict the Catholic Church as a stabilizing institution, he lauded its recognition of the interdependency of all humanity. The comparisons with the role southern conservatives trumpeted for the institution of slavery as a basis for society continued in rapid order. Porcher conceded that the Church tended to "swell the pomp and revenue of the noble," but in its capacity to provide care for all of society, "there can be no doubt that she was then the sole guardian of all that was really dear to humanity . . . she was no less the refuge and shield of the oppressed." The Church recognized common humanity through the theoretical equality of souls. It also recognized a natural, interdependent human hierarchy here on earth: "In the wide distinction which existed between the different ranks of life, that was the only institution which felt and acknowledged fellowship with all mankind." Like the good planter, Gregory VII "felt that he was the common father of mankind." Therefore it was his solemn duty to "clothe" his institution with the strength to "make her truly the guardian of the desolate, and the refuge of the oppressed."[19]

Porcher's treatment of the Inquisition was even bolder, considering the negative view widely held by the Protestant world. While it is doubtful that good Protestant southerners relished being compared to those involved in the Inquisition, Porcher plainly saw a lesson to be taught concerning the value

and function of strong institutions during times of social and political instability. Philip II and the Spanish people truly believed that their enemies in
Europe and from Muslim Africa and Turkey were gathering for an assault on
Spain "in a common cause against Christianity," according to Porcher. He
wrote, "The sense of the Spanish people, therefore, no less than that of the
monarch, demanded the establishment of an institution which should prevent
the danger. [The Inquisition] was not an engine of persecution, but an instru-
ment of self-preservation." Perhaps responding to accusations of the South
being a contentious society, Porcher continued, "When, it may be asked, in
such emergencies, after ages of fighting, when the victory was still doubtful,
have combatants ever been known to conduct themselves with moderation
and mildness?" It was, after all, the Protestants who were the revolutionaries
of that age, and "wherever the doctrines of the Reformation had made their
appearance, civil war had followed." Whereas Porcher had in 1831 cited the
Protestant Reformation as the engine of "progress," he now sympathized
with the Spanish Catholics opting for "a prudent policy to stay the progress
of opinions which seemed to carry with them the seeds of civil commotions."
What Porcher saw as unlikely in 1831, restraining "progress," now seemed a
"prudent policy" for survival.[20]

Porcher also aimed his historical criticism at George Bancroft, whose popular interpretations dominated American historical writing in the mid-1800s.
Adopting the review form pioneered by the *Edinburgh Review* (and available
among Charleston's intellectual community), the conservative Porcher criticized Bancroft as "the partisan and apologist of democracy."[21] In addition to
being an apologist for democracy, Bancroft provoked Porcher on a number of
other points. Porcher felt that Bancroft was "too ambitious" in his quest for
literary greatness; took Bancroft to task for using sloganeering rhetoric, saying, "His opinions are expressed as if he were stumping his way through an
election canvass"; and noted incredulously that Bancroft's popularizing, pleas-
ing style had made him "a fixed fact in the United States. He is authority."[22] But
more than complaining about Bancroft's style, Porcher determined to show
the weaknesses in Bancroft's faith in democracy and the common man.
Porcher argued that Bancroft's "partisan democratic zeal" caused him to "discover in every unimportant act the influence of its wise and far-reaching policy." Conversely, Bancroft castigated anyone who had impeded democracy's
glorious march. For example, Bancroft criticized harshly Samuel Johnson's
Revolutionary War–era pamphlet "Taxation No Tyranny," which defended
British policy. To Porcher it seemed that Bancroft overlooked the plain fact

that Johnson represented the ruling party in England. Therefore Bancroft's assessment was "destitute of logic as it certainly is of charity." Johnson, declared Porcher, "despite his prejudices, his absurdities and his monstrous political principles," was nonetheless a "high-minded, generous and noble man." The point here was not simply that Bancroft had demeaned the memory of Samuel Johnson. Porcher saw Bancroft's interpretation as the product of narrow, democratic, American interests similar to the histories written for narrow, Protestant interests. It distorted the full, complex life of Samuel Johnson much in the same way the spread of democracy reduced serious issues of governance to matters of partisanship and, he would argue elsewhere, the way classical economics reduced human value to the cash nexus.[23]

It is not surprising that the two historians offered contrasting views of American independence. Bancroft saw American independence as the dramatic birth of freedom, the end result of rational decisions made by a democratically inclined people. As a southern conservative, Porcher did not trust "the people." His historical interpretation of independence reflected his antidemocratic convictions. Viewing neither the people nor their leaders in the 1770s as agitating on behalf of democracy, Porcher redefined in midsentence the final break between the American colonists and England, writing that "the revolution, that is, the independence of the country, was rather forced upon us by the rashness of the agents of England" and adding that independence was not "the reflective determination of the people."[24] Too much boasting of American independence—making "ourselves the central point"—and too much disabusing of the nation's colonial past did not bode well for a conservative such as Porcher. Selected to give a eulogy to John C. Calhoun at the College of Charleston, Porcher in 1850 drew the mourners' attention to the conservative lessons of the French Revolution. "Eagerly grasping at something new" and "pursuing . . . an ideal good," the leaders of the revolution "struck at the root of all existing national institutions, and failed." The result was anarchy and bloodshed.[25]

The democratic interpretations and the popularity of Bancroft, promoted and published by northern publishers, worried Porcher and other southern conservatives and likely inspired the creation of the South Carolina Historical Society in 1857. Despite its creation late in the sectional crisis, the South Carolina Historical Society was not a fire-eater vehicle for secession. Among its more prominent original members were James Louis Petigru and George S. Bryan, erstwhile proslavery Unionists. As a tribute to his reputation within the Charleston intellectual community, Porcher was selected to deliver the keynote address at the inaugural meeting. The occasion gave Porcher the opportunity to spell out his concerns over the persisting worship of democracy and the willful American ignorance of history.

In his 1857 address Porcher congratulated South Carolina for its sturdy, republican history. No doubt preaching to the converted, Porcher explained that "partisan" histories of democracy (such as Bancroft's) exemplified the inherent weaknesses in democracy itself. Having by now moved far from his 1831 celebration of a people having broken from their past, Porcher complained that the expanding American democracy "undervalues History": "Entirely engrossed in the cares of to-day, she pays small regard to the future, and is altogether heedless of the past. Indifferent to all family ties and relationships of kindred, she takes little interest in tracing the rise of those relationships or the originals of those times." South Carolina republicanism, on the other hand, "is based upon the idea of a family connexion. A common ancestry, a common history, the recollections of adversities shared, and triumphs enjoyed; all these link together the members of a republic, and combine to make it the most stable form of government which the world has ever seen."[26] Within Porcher's assessment is the implication that stable governments and societies were in essence a fait accompli. Either a people already had a common link to the past and therefore the foundation for republican stability, or they did not and therefore would always be susceptible to the short-sightedness and instability of a democracy.

Despite having posited a safe conservative foundation for South Carolina based on its past, Porcher revealed a conflicted mind about the present, believing that "it was not, in the nature of things, possible for any other but a democracy to exist in North America."[27] Here Porcher confronted one of the many challenges proslavery writers faced in their opposition to an expanding democratic and free-labor world. Conservative South Carolinians rested their case on a belief that their state represented the fruits of a stable history, regardless of the democratic fever gripping the rest of the nation. If the course of history, however, ran with democracy, how would South Carolinians preserve their stable society and its conservative history?

Porcher also ran into problems explaining the alleged unity of South Carolina society in the late 1850s. Through the overthrow of South Carolina's proprietary government in 1719 and the Revolutionary War of the 1770s, he noted, South Carolinians "appeared to develope [*sic*] a common family, out of the discordant elements which had met on our soil." But, he continued, "How this was done, does not clearly appear." Porcher surprisingly suggested a process of "forgetting" that pointedly rejected the past and allowed South Carolinians to unite—no doubt a suggestion he would have been quick to criticize in champions of democracy such as Bancroft: "Forgetting all recollection of former discords, of former jealousies, it may be of former antipathies, all unite now around the altar of common country, and recognize no holier, no more endearing name than the common name of Carolinian." In the end Porcher tried to argue it both ways. "Forgetting" allowed South Carolinians to come together to form their republic, but "recollections of adversities shared, and triumphs enjoyed" were required to keep their republican home pure. By 1860 Porcher left his readers uncertain about the future of republicanism but amply warned that democracy threatened.[28]

Porcher's analysis of George Bancroft, the medieval Catholic Church, the legacy of the Protestant Reformation, and South Carolina republicanism all formed parts of his personal project to consider again his understanding of history. His historical work formed the foundation for his perspective on the troubled present. Porcher's critique of industrialization and liberalism in the late antebellum years reflected the increasing defensiveness and sophistication that many southern writers exhibited as they evaluated their slave society's place within the expanding free-labor world. He concluded again, as in 1831, that separation would save the South. This time, however, separation would save South Carolina from, rather than for, a world of progress through the rationalism at the heart of bourgeois liberalism and classical economics.

From the buoyant faith in progress displayed in 1831—"there can be no resisting the truth," he wrote, that time brought with it "a corresponding progress" of the rational mind—Porcher by the 1850s was wary of "what is called progress." As Eugene Genovese has written, "The dizzying outcome of the Mexican War, with its enormous territorial annexations, the projection of American power into the Pacific, and the discovery of gold in California, deepened the sense of progress, indeed of rapid progress, as the controlling law of modern civilization."[29] Progress, Porcher now worried, "is in everybody's mouth; progress is in everybody's heart; to stand still is to die."[30] In their defense of slavery, southern conservatives of the 1850s frequently pointed to the disastrous results of industrialization and free-market morality. Porcher, however, looked within liberal thought itself and offered an insightful critique on the limits as well as the conforming, sweeping intellectual power behind the modern worship of progress, utility, and change. Porcher cited Francis Bacon and Adam Smith as having cleared the way for a "new philosophy which was destined to absorb all others in its comprehensive grasp."[31] Human thought in the past century, Porcher observed, had become "decidedly practical." But despite its "apparent sympathy with humanity and its interests," bourgeois liberalism created a "school of political economy" that "imperiously demands that by her standard alone shall be judged every act and every opinion of mankind."[32] Herein lay the crux of Porcher's running critique of bourgeois liberalism through the 1850s. As James Henry Hammond had condemned free-labor ideology's "ostensive privileges and its dismal servitude," Porcher argued that despite its proclamations of freedom and progress, bourgeois liberalism actually constrained individual thought and subsequent action in narrow, tragic ways.[33] Liberal ideology in practice was guilty, he charged, of dangerously flattening the complexity of life to a few base principles.

Porcher held that the expanding capitalist world, despite its supremely confident outlook and its admittedly dynamic powers, was "internally in a state of uncertainty if not total anarchy": "The great points along whereon it unfolds itself are vague, undefined, unsatisfactory, contradictory. We know not for a certainty what is rent, how it is distinguished from profit; we are left in doubt as to the nature of capital; we do not know how to distinguish accurately between labour and capital, and to this day it has failed to give us any clear notion of the nature, use, and actual value of money."[34] As Eugene Genovese argued in *The Slaveholders' Dilemma,* slave owners' conservatism could not reject the material or the intellectual strengths of bourgeois liberalism completely out of hand.[35] Porcher offers more proof of this point. He did not deny that the market system hastened scientific and technological advances. His concern in the 1850s remained on "the evil of this philosophy," which he identified as the "extreme deduction of its principles" to profits, to accumulation, and to aggregation.[36]

As evidence of this "extreme deduction" in practice, Porcher described the seventeenth- and eighteenth-century enclosure movements in Scotland. With Scottish landowners seizing the opportunities presented by greater access to European wool-buying markets, the enclosure movement often replaced hundreds of tenant farmers with thousands of grazing sheep. Porcher noted that Scottish landowners were "in obedience to the dictates of enlightened economy . . . and the old Celtic inhabitants compelled to retire before the brutes." To their credit, he continued, compassionate people responded through the limited avenues of amelioration within the free-market system—mainly, alms. When "charity is requested, they [the wealthy] respond." Porcher's point was subtle yet powerful. In addition to causing dislocation, relentless uncertainty, and intense poverty for most people, a free-labor market society reduced the possibilities of human inter-action. The narrow range of choices offered by a market-driven economy both produced human hardship and limited the ways in which suffering was addressed. Should a landowner moved by "romantic sentiment" deny himself the maximal use of his own land as prescribed by the logic of the market system? Since the landowner always faced the potential reversal of his own well-being, Porcher admitted that one may as "reasonably deny to the manu-facturer the use of the agency of steam, or break up the printing press in order that the scribe may flourish." The language of classical economics that sanctioned the landowner's decision read "the same lessons to the poor; it is impartial in its instructions; but the lesson is a mockery to the poor man."[37]

In the British government's response to pleas for unemployment relief in the early 1830s Porcher found another example of restrictions the free-market system placed on decent, moral people. British officials argued that the cause of the unemployed was beyond the aid of government since wages depended on the supply and demand of workers. Porcher showed how the British government shifted the blame of poverty on the poor, claiming that "their own numbers were the cause of their misfortune." The government's advice to the British worker, he paraphrased, was "diminish your numbers and you will improve your condition." Porcher summarized the British gov-ernment's response succinctly and with disgust: "[It] was . . . in effect but to tell them to go home and die." As chilling as this conclusion was, it also proved to Porcher that "the moral arm of capital is drawn from the armory of the political philosophy"; in other words, he explained, given the prevail-ing logic of capitalism, "I do not know that it was in their power to give any other answer." Porcher therefore declined the invitation to "join in singing praises to the superior happiness of the present age."[38] It was one thing to rec-ognize, as Porcher also did, that in every society some prospered over others, but it was another to accept that "the accumulation of millions in one hand can be of the least possible advantage to the thousands whose wages are kept at a rate just above the point of absolute want."[39]

Porcher charged that the logic of the market had even penetrated Christ-ian thought. An Episcopalian, he observed the closeness between liberal ideol-ogy and a newer evangelical Protestantism: "How easily do Christian morals accommodate themselves to the business habits of a people; and how suddenly do we endeavour to believe that our reading is the true one because we hope it is so, or it suits our interest to have it so." Always mindful of the present crisis facing the South, Porcher brought this point home to his fellow southerners: "Opinions change daily, almost hourly, and the paradox of today is the faith of tomorrow. When Rousseau was howling out from his lair of infidelity the ominous notes of abolition, the Orthodox Christians of that age little fancied that within a century the defence [*sic*] of slavery on religious grounds, would by a large party of honest Christians, be regarded as a delusion of the arch enemy. A great deal of the Christianity now taught by reverend professors (preachers of the Beecher or Theo. Parker school, for example) would have put to shame the irreverent infidelity of Voltaire." [40] Modern morals, ethics, and religious leadership had all been transformed into a new orthodoxy among Christians. Christianity had succumbed to the "decidedly practical" philosophy of the age. Porcher summed up with bitter irony the malleability of contemporary Christianity: "If the devil ever laughs, I imagine his cachinnations must be immoderate when he witnesses the dexterity with which political economy harmonizes her instructions with those of holy writ." [41]

The rational values of "political economy" had not only "harmonized" with the modern mind and soul, they had, Porcher feared, taken them over. While in his 1831 address Porcher explained how the Puritan mind "yielded to . . . education" and "softened into a laudable desire for rational liberty," in the late 1850s the human mind, it seemed, was not so easily guided toward such positive ends: "Infinite are the sources of error," he argued, even in "the best regulated minds."[42] Northern wealth, for instance, had deluded its beneficiaries to the point where that "which a well regulated mind regards as a means, is idolatrously worshipped as an end, and wealth and worth are synonymous." [43] Extending the point further, Porcher reached the fundamentally conservative conclusion that the ever-present potential for error and danger in one mind writ large meant that "society itself is a source of error." [44] Nonetheless, he feared, an inability or unwillingness to think beyond the parameters of bourgeois liberalism persisted. In Porcher's view, even some of the era's greatest thinkers—both supporters and critics of liberalism—failed to see beyond its limits. Porcher considered John Stuart Mill an enlightened, if errant, economist of the time. In his *Principles of Political Economy,* which first appeared in 1848, Mill suggested that "restraint on population is indispensable, to prevent the increase of numbers from outstripping the increase of capital, and the condition of the classes who are at the bottom of society from being deteriorated."[45] In an insightful, if condescending, comment on the human sex drive and the hopelessness of the poor, Porcher derided Mill's argument: "So upwards of twenty millions of people, oppressed by poverty and labour, with that unthrift which is always the result of hopelessness, are to adopt a system which they cannot understand, to forego the one enjoyment which nature provides for them, which instinct urges upon them, and of which even poverty itself cannot deprive them." Such a plan forced the poor to "renounce the natural desire for conjugal and parental enjoyment, in order that the rest may enjoy them without suffering."[46]

Thomas Carlyle, never to be confused with an apologist of classical economics, surveyed the same problems as Mill did and, according to Porcher, offered planned emigration and universal education as two different solutions. Emigration of "hordes of Irish," Porcher stressed, had not lessened the severity of overpopulation and misery in Ireland and had only added to the problems of English cities. A planned relocation, he continued, would be enormously difficult to accomplish and "would doubtless be most eagerly opposed by the capitalists." Emigration allowed, or even furthered, the disruption of families already under assault by industrialization by encouraging the poor to "voluntarily cut themselves off from their common humanity." Carlyle's advocacy of universal education, which presumably would educate the poor toward better health and opportunity, was a short-sighted solution. Instead of arguing directly against education for the poor, Porcher cleverly turned the issue into another criticism of the powerful leaders of bourgeois society. The efficacy of education, he suggested, had been overstated. In a passage still worth considering, Porcher wrote that "too much is expected of education": "It is expected to work wonders for the poor; does it work wonders for the rich? Does it influence them as a body, to make any sacrifice for the common cause? Has it led them to think that the evil lies as much with them as with the poor, and has it suggested to them a reformation of their own class?"[47]

Within industrializing societies, "unceasing, bustling industry stands at the head of the virtues, and any indulgence or relaxation from labour is denounced as laziness."[48] According to Porcher, the obsession with becoming wealthy was a problem: "The love of gain which properly controlled is a blessing, has in our day become a frenzy." The drive for accumulation created a people riddled with uncertainty who, aware of the tenuousness of their own position, were driven instead to locate society's ills in the working class. They have "devised every remedy for [workers], but have utterly failed to seek for one in themselves. All the fault cannot lie on one side of the controversy." The capitalist understood too well the competitive reality of pitting himself against his fellow capitalists. The capitalist, however, failed to understand the implications of this competition for the poor. The worker went to join "that great army" which "becomes more weak as it gains in strength, and when he complains of his hard lot, he is told, and truly told, that his case is hopeless." But according to the new economic theories, "no injury is done to anyone." When "capital engages in a skirmish with capital," the deadly game "results at last in riveting still more the chains by which it binds labour to its hopeless task." It was, for Porcher, "a fearful spectacle to behold thousands of men deprived of the means of earning an honest livelihood because a few capitalists chose to battle with each other." [49]

With the traumatic change in social relations produced by the capitalist economy, Porcher feared that a traditional, organic civil society was being torn apart: "The day that cash payment for work done became the system, was the last of the old feudal social dependence." As Charleston was itself experiencing a significant rise in its white working-class population, Porcher foresaw a day when workers would become "a fourth order in the state, with a rapid tendency to the character of a hostile one. It is all important that the antagonism shall not become of actual hostility." If that day came, it threatened "a revolution more terrible than any yet witnessed by the world." He warned that it could not be God's will that "his creatures shall exist in hopeless degradation, toiling harder than slaves, with none of the slave's security for repose when the night shall come in which he cannot work." Finally reaching a crescendo of condemnation, Porcher called the philosophical foundation of liberalism "the offspring of the devil. . . . It is devilish in its origin, devilish in its results, and devilish will be the catastrophe which shall overturn it." [50]

It took decades for proslavery intellectuals to formulate their critiques of capitalist economics and bourgeois liberal ideology. Ironically, the more they learned about capitalism and political liberalism, the more they were haunted by the fear that there was little that they, the leaders of this slave-based society poised on the periphery of the capitalist world, could do about it. The southern elite, according to Porcher, as leaders of a hierarchical, organic, paternalistic society, were unwilling to accept the capitalist's hopeless view of the poor or capitalism's disastrous effects on traditional social relations. "Slavery," Porcher proclaimed, was the "essential element in Southern civilization."[51] The peculiar institution was the foundation from which other purportedly natural hierarchies in the plantation community sprang. The South, he noted, was "not yet engulphed [*sic*] in the great maelstrom caused by the workings of political philosophy." Even this position was tenuous, however. The slave South, Porcher worried, was not immune to "the law of society" that made the human family "the sharer of each other's fortunes." The best the South could hope for were policies that softened "the force of the blow . . . and the extreme pains of the catastrophe."[52] The dilemma within proslavery thought could not be made any clearer. The slave made the South, for the moment, different and unique within the liberalizing Euro-American world; but the southerner's humanity and the South's history linked them inseparably to those other members of God's family in the North and in Europe, where inexorably, they feared, the laws of political economy continued to work.

Porcher also understood the powerful logic behind free-labor ideology that had not only narrowed the view of the past and present but had set parameters on language itself. Showing powerful insight, he wrote, "Our whole fabric of society is based upon slave institutions, and yet our conventional language is drawn from scenes totally at variance with those which lie about us."[53] As Elizabeth Fox-Genovese has written, "Because of the continuity of the vocabulary of individualism and freedom, notably in the language of republicanism, it did not immediately become apparent [to antebellum southern fiction writers] that the individualism that was unfolding in bourgeois societies represented the absolute antithesis of slavery."[54] Living in the midst of the southern crisis of the mid-nineteenth century, Porcher witnessed this revelation. "What then are we to do when our needs require a new word?" he asked searchingly.[55]

Porcher's uncertain handling of how exactly southern society should relate to the rest of the world revealed further the southern intellectual's dilemma. In the late 1850s he cast about for different alternatives for the South's future. Porcher held that since the slave "has stamped us with conservatism," the South could not enter into the "race of progress" consuming northern society. His solution, however, did not require that the slave South therefore reject the modern world, but that "our pace must be a slow one."[56] Porcher, in essence, suggested that somehow the slave South should be in, but not of, the emerging, market-driven, "civilized" world. Elsewhere he predicted that the United States would not avoid the problems that plagued England: "There is no reason to hope that she will not in time come in for her full share of all its terrible results."[57] Here Porcher argued for separation: "The philosophy of the North is a dead letter to us. The doctrines of political economy are not true here." He called southern thinkers to the intellectual task at hand, claiming, "Our philosophy has yet to be developed."[58]

Porcher's hopes for the South ultimately rested on faith that the wisdom he believed inherent in a slave society would prevail. He contended that the North remained "tossed about by every wind of political doctrine, agitated by the alluring light of a meretricious philosophy which is slowly but remorselessly gnawing the vitals of her social system." Driven by the "spirit of gain to the utmost of industrial development," the North lay in greater danger than the South.[59] Meanwhile, for the South, Porcher speculated that "when the day of general reckoning shall come, they will perhaps, be found least deficient, which have not sacrificed everything to the cause of progress."[60] Men, after all, "do not practice falsehood for its own sake." Soon, he hoped, "the mists of prejudice" would "lift themselves from the fallacies which they protected."[61] Indeed a day of general reckoning came for slave-owning conservatives such as Frederick Porcher.

CHAPTER TWO

I Shook Off My Slumber

Frederick Porcher and the Postwar Conservative View

Following the Civil War, Frederick Porcher continued to teach in Charleston, where it seemed that the Old South, his world, was unmistakably gone: "To the Old Carolinian, everything was strange—everything was so different from old customs and practices. . . . As he looked bewildered around him and about him, he felt he had become a stranger, that he had no home."[1] Porcher's lament, deepened no doubt by the death in October 1865 of his son Edward, was understandable, if short-lived. The southern elite had to contend with the inescapable fact that the society they had led into civil war lay beaten and defeated. Porcher experienced firsthand the hardships of defeat and the social confusion caused by emancipation even before the war ended. In December 1864 he wrote to Judah P. Benjamin, the Confederate secretary of state and an old college classmate, advocating the arming of slaves. "If the negro is to be employed in the war let him be employed for our defense and protection and not our destruction," he reasoned, adding, "the soldiers who fight our battles must of course be free."[2] With the war finally over, Porcher in May 1865 lined up alongside former slaves to receive food and supplies from the local commissary. "It was a grand day for the negroes," his daughter Clelia wrote, but Porcher also came away with "five hams, a barrel of molasses, and some sole leather."[3]

Antebellum southern conservatism and elite rule rested on a foundation of slave ownership.[4] Recent books by Manisha Sinha and Charles B. Dew remind readers once again of the deep, abiding commitment southern conservatives had to the institution of slavery.[5] After the war, moreover, there was never any doubt that men such as Frederick Porcher would somehow remain "conservative." But upon what now would their worldview rest? Porcher's lectures show that he adapted antebellum notions of racial hierarchy, elite rule, and the "authority of history" to an emerging laissez-faire economic conservatism found in Gilded Age America.[6] For Porcher, the Civil War came to represent the ultimate confrontation between two economic systems—and free-labor capitalism had won. This interpretation of the war places Porcher's conservatism apart from the views of other postwar southern conservatives such as Robert L. Dabney or Albert Taylor Bledsoe. Dabney and Bledsoe often interpreted the war as a clash of moral systems—an agnostic North versus a Christian South.[7] Porcher, unlike many other southern conservatives, managed to avoid much of the seemingly endless postwar debate over which side, the North or the South, had done a better job of interpreting the Constitution and the Bible.

Emancipation in the lowcountry of South Carolina produced one of the most severe testing grounds of African American freedom in the former Confederacy. In addition to its aristocratic slave-owning class, the lowcountry featured a large black population shaped over the years by a rice plantation culture that fostered slave autonomy.[8] Throughout most of the war Union troops occupied much of the Carolina coast, but they did not capture Charleston until early 1865. The lowcountry elite were among the few former Confederates to have land confiscated by the national government and redistributed to the former slaves, though this policy was soon overturned by Andrew Johnson. Fire-damaged Charleston became home to a growing black community after the war. Bernard E. Powers Jr. points out that Charleston's black population increased by nearly ten thousand between 1860 and 1870.[9] With passage of the Reconstruction Acts in 1867 stipulating ratification of the Fourteenth Amendment for reentry into the Union, white Charlestonians watched as an emerging black political leadership met and produced what became the constitution of 1868, securing citizenship and suffrage for black men. As a witness to all this, Frederick Porcher in almost every way conceivable saw his world turned upside down: African Americans were free; democracy had expanded to include black men; and the federal government through its Reconstruction Acts and military presence shaped daily life in South Carolina.

Porcher's fellow conservatives countered nascent black political organization with meetings and announcements of their own. As late as November 1867 the *Charleston Daily Courier* saw fit to remind its white readers, "Slavery is at an end"; white Charlestonians would not resurrect slavery now because "it is too late to correct the error of its sudden extinction."[10] Postwar realities left no room for considerations of actual reenslavement. Relinquishing the view that slavery was a sanctioned institution needed for social order marked a significant change in the conservative ideology. Porcher explained in his 1850 eulogy to Calhoun the conditions under which change could occur. While

establishing that "existing institutions are sacred," Porcher conceded the likelihood of having to "apply those wholesome correctives which necessity may
require, and circumstances indicate."[11] Porcher certainly did not consider
emancipation as a wholesome corrective, but there was little doubt that
necessity and circumstances had intervened. Or, as Porcher wrote on another
matter, "It is astonishing how soon we get accustomed to any state of things."[12]
While slavery was considered a dead issue, much of the Old South conservative catechism survived. A November 1867 convention of conservatives in
Charleston outlined the postwar conservative beliefs. Local rule through states'
rights, white supremacy, and the fear of democracy all survived the war. The
convention also gave hints of a developing industrial-age conservatism cher-
ishing property rights and accepting as unavoidable the labor/capital antagonism of a capitalist economy.

In its postwar defense of the states' rights philosophy, the conservative
convention granted that the emergency of war necessitated that the federal
government reign "supreme." But, as the *Charleston Daily Courier* reported, "Is
this *law*, or is this usurpation? Is this good government, or is it revolution?" A
strong central government during a crisis of war was one thing. Conservatives
asked if South Carolinians were now willing to endorse "so monstrous a
proposition into our government polity." Calhoun could not have stated any
clearer the states' rights view that conservative South Carolinians still held in
1867: "To admit as a fact, as has been assumed to be the result of the war, that
the Government of the United States is supreme, and that the States have no
rights; or, if they have rights, that they are subordinate to the Government of
the United States; or, which is the same thing, subordinate to the will of a
majority having control of the Government, is to admit the abrogation of the
Constitution, and to ignore the facts of history."[13]

Centralization of political power at the national level, especially with
the inclusion of black voters, was the opening wedge leading to other revolutions. Black citizenship sanctioned by the federal Constitution upset conservative notions of local rule and natural racial hierarchy. Against this,
conservatives voiced "their most solemn protest." Invoking a three-way
explanation for white supremacy, they asserted that in his inferiority "the
black man is what God and nature and circumstances have made him." It was,
therefore, not his fault that "the negro is utterly unfitted to exercise the highest functions of the citizen."[14]

While South Carolina's elite suffered heavy financial loss with emancipation,
they still held their land. Moreover, if the elite did not enjoy the prosperity

of earlier days, they understood fully that as property holders they occupied an advantageous position relative to the former slaves. Consequently property rights remained a matter of critical importance to postwar conservatives. The recent political empowerment of another non-property-holding segment of society was not just a blow to white supremacy; it suggested looming class conflict as well. This was not the first time Charleston's conservatives voiced their fears of a growing working class. In the 1850s the city's white working-class population rose significantly. This development prompted Christopher Memminger to complain to James H. Hammond that "every one of them would have a vote," while Alfred Huger weighed in before the war with the opinion that those "who have no property are already sufficiently willing to be Enemies of those who have."[15]

The Reconstruction Acts, conservatives argued, placed the power to tax "in the hands of those who own no property," while it took power away from "those who hold the property and must pay the taxes." To them, this was not just a bad idea but a dangerous one. "The war," they warned, "that has always existed between capital and labor is decided in favor of the latter." This spelled trouble for all property holders, not just white Southerners: "The wealth of the country is prostrated at the feet of those who have nothing at stake but their daily wages and their daily bread." A government that reflected the needs of the propertyless was surely to follow, and the end, conservatives predicted, would be "practical confiscation of the small remaining substance of our people." The conservative convention's statement ended with a flourish: "In the name, then, of humanity to both races—in the name of *citizenship* under the Constitution—in the name of a common history in the past— in the name of our Anglo-Saxon race and blood—in the name of the civilization of the nineteenth century—in the name of magnanimity and the noble instincts of manhood—in the name of God and nature, we protest against these Acts, as destructive to the peace of society, the prosperity of the country, and the greatness and grandeur of our common future."[16]

Still teaching at the College of Charleston, Frederick Porcher began rebuilding his own sense of order by conceding that indeed the slave South had been "engulphed" by the "great maelstrom" of bourgeois liberalism and capitalism.[17] In his antebellum writings Porcher had already wondered if the slave South would be able to hold the modern economic revolution at bay. Obviously by 1865 the answer was no. But, as Porcher discovered, this concession to the power of capitalist economic forces opened up new interpretive possibilities for the conservative viewpoint. For instance, Porcher used this position to remove blame for the South's defeat from the region's conservative leadership. In a postwar lecture to his students at the College of Charleston on the demise of the city's slaveholding elite, he taught that "it was not they [the planters] but the entire system" that was to blame for the subsequent disaster of the 1860s and that the slave-plantation economy was "destined" to break up the Union and be destroyed as a "principle of political economy."[18] Porcher recounted how debt had forced him out of the planting business before the war, and he associated his failure with the fate of the slave society. "I was a bad planter, a bad master, a bad manager," he admitted, recalling that as a planter, "I felt myself . . . becoming inefficient, indifferent; my energy was leaving me."[19] In the 1840s his friend and fellow intellectual William Gilmore Simms had asked Porcher to contribute to Simms's publication *Magnolia*. Porcher declined, noting later that his mind had become "stagnant." He explained that he "was spell-bound" because "that unfortunate plantation of mine was making me a poor man."[20] Porcher linked his power to think with his role as a planter. His loss of intellectual sophistication, he suggested, was symptomatic of life in a slave society, implicating the best people of the South and their capacity to lead their society. Yet he concluded that the fault was not entirely his. He stated, "Of all the occupations of this life I suppose that of a planter . . . is the best calculated to lead to ruin," but he explained that, fortunately, "I shook off my slumber" and moved on to a more stimulating, productive life.[21] As for the planter class as a whole, the destruction of slavery, he hoped, would awaken other slumbering planters to the realization that as members of a class they remained worthy of their elite status.

Porcher found no contradiction in judging the lost slave society a failure and its slave-owning elite a success, since he now saw the South's defeat in hindsight as inevitable. He wrote that the influence of the planter class in South Carolina was "universal and felt even where not suspected"; that its members did not "move in the first rank" of innovators and were, rather, "decidedly conservative"; and that as such, "in the mad race of the nineteenth century" their conservatism remained a positive influence to South Carolina.[22] Porcher in 1850 went so far as to proclaim that "greatness" itself was "essentially conservative."[23] Writing now amidst white southern allegations of corruption by South Carolina's Reconstruction government, he stressed that the planter class left a legacy in society and politics that was "not only clean but brilliant"; that as a people they were the "salt of Society which they kept pure and clean"; and that as "God fearing and God serving," they were "men of honour and honourable men."[24]

In his memoirs (written shortly after the war even though Porcher lived until 1888), the depiction of the planter's poor white neighbors contrasts sharply from his 1857 vision of a South Carolina society based upon "the idea of a family connexion" and where "a common ancestry, a common history, the recollections of adversities shared, and triumphs enjoyed" linked together all members of that republican state.[25] Recollections of his childhood years included memories of poor whites in the family's Cedar Spring plantation neighborhood. As a boy Porcher learned to distinguish his family's planter friends from "the people . . . in a humbler walk of life" by the clothes and "closely cropped hair of the other people"; and he confessed that "of the other people I knew nothing, and fear was the result of ignorance." Wagons bound for Charleston passed by Cedar Spring, and here too Porcher could determine which were of the elite and which were not: "I looked with dread upon those wagons [of the poor], I suppose I had been told that they had bad boys under their tents. The Wagoners looked so unlike the men I was accustomed to see, travel stained, rough, uncouth."[26]

Porcher's postwar defense of the lowcountry's organization into parishes —an arrangement that lasted until the defeat of the Confederacy, which gave the lowcountry an inordinate amount of political power versus the upcountry—also reflected his fears of those white and black locals not of the elite class. The parish system, he conceded, was "anomalous, illogical, and perhaps irrational." But from Porcher's perspective it suited the needs of his conservative family, friends, and neighbors: "If it had no other good result, it staved off for a long time that flood of unbridled democracy which has submerged all the other states, and which I suppose will soon engulf us also in its relentless abyss."[27]

Porcher's memories of the religious differences in the neighborhood also ran along class lines. His Episcopalian Church, with its "calmness and seriousness" of ritual, fit the intellectual climate established by the planter class. The liturgy was "acceptable to the best taste" while "applicable to every condition of humanity." Methodism, on the other hand, represented a contrasting, shocking element within the community. The local Methodists appeared to the Porcher family's circle "strange, grotesque and objects rather of ridicule than of respect." The Methodist service included "contortions of body" and "the interruptions of the prayer or the sermon by the ejaculations of the congregation." The singing was "entuned richly with a strong nasal articulation, almost every stanza being terminated with a refrain of the most grotesque character." The effect "failed to produce on the minds of the really serious any feeling beyond that of pity and regret, that such should be the handmaid of religion." Of course this emotional appeal to the Lord resonated locally with the poor, including a distant relative of Porcher, upon whom "fortune had not smiled, . . . on the contrary she had frowned," he noted. None in this poor family "had the strength of character which assists in bearing up under adversity." Porcher explained how, predictably, class resentment sank in and how "such persons almost invariably proclaim war against the prosperous." Lacking character and at war against the wealthy, the relatives became Methodists. Methodism "made so little distinction between the laity and the clergy" that it could "so easily exalt the open sinner into the teacher's seat" and "appeared to them a panacea for all their woes."[28]

Writing of his days as a college professor before the war, Porcher recalled unhappily a greater presence at the College of Charleston of evangelical Christians in the last antebellum years: "I used to say that I was afraid of every pious lad except those who belonged to the Episcopal Church. In that Church, piety is not allowed to be so demonstrative as in the more democratic Protestant Churches." Porcher singled out the "Junior Class of 1855" especially, lumping together "several disorderly members" with those "who had an outside reputation for piety." Sizing up the composition of the class, Porcher predicted trouble: "I have lived to learn that whenever one has a reputation for [piety], that he presumes upon it, and is a dangerous member of society. The piety that makes capital of itself is dangerous."[29]

Porcher used his history lectures to address the new political power of the black community. As Thomas Holt has noted, over half of South Carolina's state and federal officeholders during Reconstruction were African American, and the black majority in the state house of representatives was two-to-one during the same years.[30] Porcher's estimation of African Americans, not surprisingly, remained unchanged from his days as a slave owner. "A great experiment," Porcher observed, "is now making in this country to commit the highest responsibilities of civilization to a race which in its native soil has never shown any capacity for improvement. You who hear me will be able to witness the result." Porcher, however, guided his young students with the strong suggestion that it, too, would fail: "Civilization is an Innate Faculty, not an acquired Habit. It is a gift of God, not the result of human teaching."[31]

Porcher's lesson on the slave in contact with "civilization" foretold a difficult future for postwar African American political activity in South Carolina in the midst of white resistance. Even under the tutelage of the master's civilization, he wrote, the slave had "not advanced far beyond the state in which he was when brought in contact with civilization." Porcher pushed the point further: "What civilization he has acquired is the direct gift of slavery, and though he has learned the language of civilization he has not learned to make language a true vehicle of his thought." In essence Porcher rejected in one sweeping statement the intellectual validity of any political voice coming from the African American community. The former slave, he argued, lacked the capacity to utilize this "true vehicle" of language. African American political activity, therefore, was better seen as a crude expression of the freedman's political liberty, which Porcher made clear meant "the right to vote as his leaders or governors direct him."[32]

Having denied African Americans the capacity to speak in terms of "civilization," he further denied them the capacity to speak against their former masters. African American leaders wielded considerable influence at times over opposing white Democrats but also over their white Republican colleagues.[33] Black workers resisted land restoration to former white owners, onerous task work arrangements, and low wages.[34] Porcher, however, felt certain that African American words of protest were "not spontaneous utterings, but were put into their mouths by the sickly and unprincipled adventurers who lived upon the white men and made use of the negroes to aid in robbing them." From prewar "relations of kindness" to postwar "evil passions," Porcher employed contrasting characterizations of African Americans depending on how they related to him and his class. "Negro fiends" could be easily stirred to riot by "sickly and unprincipled" whites, but when faced with an organized body of proper whites, men such as himself, they became "completely overawed."[35]

In the heat of national Reconstruction efforts to guarantee political rights for the former slaves, Porcher countered that the African American's apparent loss of liberty in slavery was just that—apparent. "He suffered no privation" of rights, Porcher insisted, stepping for the moment outside the reach of the Enlightenment, "for he had none in the country from which he was brought." Porcher further asserted that the slaves made no effort to change their condition of servitude. Even as Yankee soldiers approached, "they cheerfully stood and in the absence of their masters on military duty faithfully took care of his interest."[36] This passage is especially revealing considering that the Porcher family, like many other slaveholding families, experienced problems with slave discipline during the war. In October 1864 Porcher's son Frederick George wrote to his stepmother, Caroline: "You really surprise me, when you tell me that Adonis has turned out to be a rascal. I always thought him one of the best, one of the honestest [sic] John [another of Porcher's sons] owned. Its [sic] really hard to tell which of your negroes you can trust."[37] Also, when lowcountry planter John Berkeley Grimball lost over seventy slaves who ran to Union lines in early 1862, Porcher carried out a letter-writing campaign to help relocate the rest of Grimball's slaves farther away from the temptation of freedom. Porcher's efforts succeeded, from Grimball's perspective, who wrote how he was "deeply grateful to the kindness of the Professor."[38]

The odds that an intelligent man like Frederick Porcher simply forgot these episodes in which his slaves and those of a friend failed to stand cheerfully with the master's family are mighty slim indeed. What, then, accounts for the discrepancy? Postwar conservatives such as Porcher believed sincerely that history would prove them worthy leaders. But living in what they considered desperate times prompted them often to leave little to chance. White militiamen intimidated, assaulted, and murdered black citizens during Reconstruction. Conservative history professors taught the sons of the elite that the slaves remained faithful in their servitude. The former resulted in political "victory" by 1877. The latter contributed to a skewed interpretation of southern history that lasted a century. Nonetheless, after the war Porcher maintained that the former slave "may seem to be emancipated, but as soon as the power that lifts him up is removed, he subsides to his natural place in Society and quietly takes the place nature has assigned to him."[39]

Privately, Porcher appeared to take a different view of how nature assigned places among the races. His daughter Anne described the highly charged atmosphere in Charleston stemming from the gubernatorial campaign of 1876, which ended Reconstruction. "Papa," Anne Porcher wrote, "says it is no longer merely political, but much deeper, people feel that it is a war of races, and the negroes are only quiet when they are conscious that the whites are vigilant"; according to her father, with the "slightest relaxation" by the whites, black Charlestonians "become obstreperous."[40] In the quiet lecture halls of the College of Charleston, Porcher taught that racial hierarchy was a result of nature's assignment. The streets of the city, however, presented a different kind of learning environment, one where violence to maintain white supremacy continued to be the lesson of the day.

As would be expected from a southern conservative, Porcher's understanding of the natural ordering of human society went beyond a simple assertion of white supremacy. His disdain of both "unprincipled adventurers" and unprincipled white men revealed his concern not merely with the return of white political rule, but also with the return of traditional white elite rule. In *The Southern Tradition at Bay,* Richard M. Weaver captures wonderfully and succinctly the conservative premise for elite rule. As Weaver writes, elite rule was justified, they believed, because "God willed it; experience proved it."[41] Frederick Porcher sided especially with the last half of that formulation. In his lectures on British history and the development of Parliament, Porcher taught that a traditional ruling elite acted as *the* crucial link between the power of the state and the desires of the people. "The Aristocracy," he wrote, "stipulates not only for itself, but for the whole nation."[42] In their successful power struggle with the king, the English elite were "obliged to call on the aid of the common people whose liberties they pledged themselves to maintain as well as their own." The result was a hierarchical, yet interdependent British society over which Porcher gushed that "the triumph of the aristocracy was also the triumph of the people and a very important step in their progress towards complete liberty."[43] In an 1876 rebuttal to a book by T. W. Fields, *Major Gardin's Anecdotes,* in which the South Carolina revolutionary governor John Rutledge was criticized for his aristocratic leanings, Porcher responded: "Whether Mr. Rutledge was or was not an aristocrat we know not. If he was, there was no great harm in it. As a sensible man, and a lover of his country, of course he detested universal suffrage. Does any honest and intelligent man in the United States think that any good has arisen out of it?"[44] The United States had, for the moment anyway, broken from its historic, British roots. Radicalism, "the principle that equality before law means, Equality in all social, moral, and intellectual qualities," had "spread her baleful influence over the land."[45] The same point showed up in another lecture in which Porcher proclaimed, "Anyone who will give humanity a thought must be struck with the inequalities which exist among men—but it takes a good deal of thought to discover that the progress of humanity depends on these inequalities."[46]

Porcher's lectures on different forms of government and their constitutions struck a particularly timely chord in postwar South Carolina. He took a significantly different approach to the matter than had former Confederates Jefferson Davis and Alexander Stephens, who were at that time piling up thousands of pages defending the South's constitutional case for secession. Porcher, on the other hand, waved off the tumultuous postwar season of state constitution writing and rewriting by invoking the importance of history in governance. "Government is a growth," he explained, "not a creation. . . . All governments are administered on the principles on which the people have grown." Americans especially, he noted, were fond of contrasting their constitutions with the British constitution: "In the former they say, Rights and Liberties are secured by written charters, while the latter is only a body of customs." Porcher insisted that they failed to understand that custom and history offered more substance than the "paper assurances" of a written constitution.[47] Porcher first expressed wariness of written constitutions in his 1831 address. Then, in a plaintive letter to Judah P. Benjamin during the war, he wrote: "In times of war and invasion the Constitution is dead. The safety of the people is the Supreme Law of the Land, superior even to the constitution."[48] To his postwar students Porcher proclaimed that had the framers of the American Constitution attempted provisions "contrary to their old unwritten customs, they would be at this moment as dead as any of those which men framed to hail the birth of Liberty in France." Hearkening back to his antebellum interpretation, the independence of the United States was a conservative movement, and "the real guarantee of newly born liberties, was the old custom of Liberty."[49] And, he might have added, the "old custom of Liberty" left most out but the propertied elite.

With South Carolina governed now through its 1868 constitution, which expanded the state's voting lists to include black men, Porcher once again turned to a contrast of democracies and republics. "In theory," he began, "the republic is the best government imaginable, the democracy one of the worst." To attack the idea of a broad-based democracy, Porcher called forward his antebellum, antidemocratic roots. He criticized the British utilitarian Jeremy Bentham for the latter's faith in simple majority rule. John C. Calhoun's influence surfaced as Porcher noted that under majority rule the minority always faced elimination, and he confessed that he did not know how "according to the principles of Bentham [the majority] could consistently refuse to proceed at once to the sacrifice." He argued that the Roman Republic fell apart when it "converted itself into a sweeping democracy." Pure democracy gave "a large field for its agitations of the demagogues." The difference was clear: "A republic is governed by laws which it is the interest of every class to maintain; a democracy is swayed by a popular leader."[50]

As the only other major regime installed through universal male suffrage, France in 1848 demonstrated for Porcher the tyrannical tendencies inherent in democracies. The French confirmed the political power of Louis Napoleon by electing him president under the new constitutional government. "It would seem that now if ever there was hope," Porcher asserted dramatically, that "France would enjoy constitutional liberty." He pointed out that France had a written constitution, adding, "that American panacea for all political evils." The new French constitution was built from "the best models by the most accomplished masters, with all the modern improvements superadded." Louis Napoleon, however, began to chafe under constitutional opposition and carried out the coup d'état of 1848. Shortly thereafter Louis Napoleon proclaimed himself Napoleon III and turned to the people to support his claim. "Thus there in the middle of the 19th Century," Porcher concluded, "in the leading state of Europe, was a gross usurpation committed, the fundamental laws of the state violated, and the usurper, true to the spirit of the age, appealed for support to the Democracy of the State." The appeal, he noted scornfully, succeeded—the French people voted that "he had done well, and solemnly invested him with despotic power."[51]

Porcher's postwar writings asserted relentlessly the values of traditional white-elite-led rule against the evils of racial egalitarianism and mass democracy. He also taught his students the history of free labor, placing it within the conservative framework of the "perpetual conflict between capital and labour, and the spirit of socialism which grows out of it." Porcher began his history of free labor by tracing the end of feudalism in England during the reign of Edward III in the 1300s. The combination of the bubonic plague that killed half of England's population and the high demand for soldiers produced a fundamental change in ancient systems of labor. The sweep of events "taught" the landed elite of Europe that "the result of free hired labour worked much more to their profit" than did the old system of "enforced duties paid by serfs." The landowners, however, were not the only ones to learn this lesson. "The labourer," Porcher noted, "had the sagacity to see his advantage and refused to work except at high wages." With a scarcity of labor and the intense competition among landowners, whose greed "added to their own injury," a volatile situation emerged. The English landlord, he wrote, "had a new problem of political economy to solve."[52]

Without using many specific historical references, Porcher taught that English landowners foolishly turned to the state to solve these new problems of a free-labor, market economy. Through legislation British landowners, not unlike South Carolina's postwar planters, sought to fix the price of labor and to prevent workers from moving. Porcher criticized English landowners for seeking redress through the hand of government and used the precedent to comment on contemporary times as well. Their efforts "showed as much wisdom as their successors have done, when after the lapse of five hundred years they still believe that natural and unavoidable evils in the social system, may be corrected by legislation." Larger economic forces "beyond the control of the government" had raised bread prices, but the English landowners "never thought of fixing and limiting the price of bread." As a result of this misguided attempt to correct "natural and unavoidable" problems of supply and demand, the laws instead increased discontent, fanned insurrection, and remained "powerless for good."[53]

From here Porcher went on to draw some sweeping, conservative conclusions that took his students from thirteenth-century England to a much newer world of international communism. "One of the last things that you can teach an average legislature," he observed, "is that it is folly to strive against nature." The best position a "wise and prudent" government could take was to "stand aside, and let labour and capital adjust their differences." With a system of government that kept its proper place outside the workings of the economy, the resolution between capital and labor would be "prompt, amicable, and permanent." Instead, the English landowners pressed for protective legislation, which "not only failed, but were mischievous and the discontents of the labouring class took the shape, which it has never since lost, of their hostility to the prosperous class and of blind and reckless communism." The laws had the doubly negative effect of demonizing the propertied class and establishing a precedent of turning to the state's power for redress of economic ills. This combination, in Porcher's mind, sounded "the first notes of that communism which is even now threatening to subvert the whole social fabric, not only in Europe but also in America." He noted mournfully that, with both sides now invoking the power of the state, "the suffering [class] produces communism and the prosperous class force." What then was government's role? Porcher's explanation places him solidly in the conservative tradition yet again: "A good government will always do mischief when it departs from its legitimate duty of protecting men in the exercise of their duties—and . . . any attempt to act directly for the benefit of the people or of any class of people and to interfere for their welfare, is a departure from its vocation and a dangerous precedent fraught with every evil which anarchy and tyranny can inflict."[54]

Porcher's traditional southern conservative belief in the fundamental inequalities within society provided the foundation for his critique of communism. If, he speculated, "men were equalized today, inequalities would be found among them tomorrow." Some would dream in this hypothetical, communist world that a golden age had arrived when "men should be neither rich nor poor, [who] would suppose also that men would need no longer work." These dreamers, however, "would soon run through their substance and become a pauper class." Porcher thought he saw evidence of this in Charleston. Much as they had in the antebellum years, South Carolina's conservatives saw and understood the events happening in their locale as part of a wider sweep of intellectual, political, and economic developments. Experiencing firsthand the free-labor world, Porcher interpreted the poverty experienced by many former slaves as, in part, the failure of the nation's egalitarian dreams now threatening property owners. As Charleston's black population swelled in the years following the war, Porcher wrote that poor black farmers "will have nothing to eat by the time winter fairly sets in. I look forward to a winter of suffering and famine. They will all flock here, and no one's property will be safe." Charleston's current black community fared little better in Porcher's estimation: "We are going to have hard times with the negroes. They are suffering from want of work, and their numbers are daily increased by people from the country, and nothing will be safe from their depredations."[55]

Porcher still recognized that the northern and English industrial economies generated unprecedented wealth for a few and massive discontent for many. Although his acceptance of capitalism's power released the planter class from blame for local devastation in the past, it carried with it disturbing international problems in the present. In surveying the postwar capitalist world, Porcher revived part of his prewar critique of capitalism—but with a significant twist. He observed that "in several countries at the present time . . . there are a few men whose wealth is so enormous as to be beyond our ordinary powers of computation, while there is an almost infinite number of men anxious for work who are not only poor men, but are steeped in poverty and wretchedness." A healthy society provided the worker with barely more than met the daily needs, thereby encouraging thrift. Porcher warned, however, that "it is certain that in neither England nor in this country is Society this happy state." There existed "discontent among labourers" and "immeasurable harshness among the patrons of labour." Struggling for a solution, Porcher concluded that "both parties are wrong."[56]

Despite blaming "both parties" in contemporary labor disputes, Porcher now granted capitalists the benefit of the doubt. He claimed that there was little that the capitalist "sailing from the full tide of prosperity" could do except remain conscious of the fact that "in the nature of things the tide must turn." Normally when this turn occurred, the capitalist tended to his own well-being, since "there is no code of ethics which calls upon him to ruin himself in order to continue a little longer the prosperity of his workmen." Modern capitalists were imperfect, he stressed, not mean-hearted. They simply failed to recognize the signs of economic downturn. Capitalists were "drawn into the vortex by the influence of a vicious system which perhaps they are unable to resist, the danger of which it is possible they did not even suspect." When danger came, capitalists must for the good of all avoid total ruin, since "no good can be done to the workman by [the capitalists] braving it, and ignoring it. They may hold out for a brief while, but if they do ruin will certainly overtake them, and bring them all, capital and labour in one common ruin."[57]

Before the war, of course, Porcher had believed that the slave South could avoid exactly this situation. His prewar analysis of bourgeois liberalism included a harsh criticism of the limited choices open to the capitalist and the hardships this created for workers. The prewar, proslavery Porcher boasted of the superiority of slave-based society over the persistent social unrest in England and the North. Porcher now used the same scenario of an economic slump and limited choices to justify, not criticize, the actions of the elite in this new world.

The working class, on the other hand, did not see all that the capitalists must consider. With complaints echoing those conservatives used elsewhere against poor voters, Porcher described the working class: "It sees its own hardship, it feels its own losses, and imagines it suffers at the will of capital." Unfortunately the worker, too, was susceptible to the passionate wiles of the demagogue. Organized labor, Porcher noted, "not only refuses to accept the terms which are offered to it, but destroys the capital in which its hopes of employment depend. It is such excesses as these that bring discredit on the labour cause and actually strengthen capital in the great conflict between capital and labour." According to Porcher, the demand of workers that their wages not be decreased was unreasonable: "They fondly suppose that a given rate of wages is just, and fancy that any thing short of that is oppression on the part of the employers." Porcher urged instead that all must accept the workings of nature. "Nature" might overproduce one year and underproduce the next. "If nature thus varies, what can be expected of human operations but that they should vary too?" Wages therefore were linked to the workings of nature and "must fall and rise to meet the ever changing complications of affairs." Therefore, he concluded, the labor movement was not fighting against capital; it was fighting a hopeless struggle against nature.[58]

A walk from the College of Charleston campus to East Bay during the immediate postwar years would have given Porcher a firsthand view of labor unrest. In 1867, 1868, 1869, and 1873 Charleston workers, white and black, struck for better wages and working conditions. The *Charleston Daily Courier* cited the "unusual spectacle" of stevedores "white and colored," making their presence and complaints known along the docks. Whether or not the stevedores imagined their suffering, as Porcher suggested in his lecture, they won some of their strikes.[59]

Porcher reiterated his theory of wages and nature to his third wife Caroline Smith Parker, using as an example an 1875 strike in Massachusetts. Workers, rather than accepting a 10 percent wage decrease, "determined to take a holiday for six weeks." During this period "they suffered greatly" and in the end were willing to return to work even at the reduced wages. The ownership, however, believing that "times had not mended with them," insisted, in addition to the lower wages, that workers "renounce all connection with the Trade Union." Porcher applauded the "master's" approach.[60]

Postwar relations between labor and capital in South Carolina also featured in Porcher's "history" of Reconstruction, published in the *Southern Historical Society Papers*. In it he described the 1876 strike among African American rice workers in the lowcountry. Not surprisingly, Porcher sided with the plantation owners. In what no doubt would have prompted a dissenting view from the rice workers, Porcher began his analysis by noting, "Whether the negroes had just grounds of complaint against their employers is a question of no moment whatever." It was, rather, "a morbid sentiment" that "endeavored to excuse them on the ground of unfair conduct on the part of the planters." As he had taught in his lectures, the impetus for agitation could not have come from the African American workers. It came from "those who, living elsewhere, were occasionally hired to assist the regular forces."[61]

Working in his new views of political economy, Porcher observed that the rice workers, as with the Massachusetts factory workers, "refused to work for such wages as were offered them, (which they had a perfect right to do)." In Porcher's view, trouble began when the workers became "lawless" and "compelled the contract hands to stop work also." Workers' collective efforts violated the fundamental premise of the individual operating within a free-labor economy. This was a "high-minded outrage," Porcher complained, "becoming so common all over the country as to be acquiring the force of unwritten law." He criticized organized labor in the same terms that he attacked the forces for democracy. Collective action by workers was "a practice which strikes at the root of all civilization, by making the will of an unreasoning mob, the superior law of the land." Since the workers' collective action fell outside Porcher's understanding of the "natural" workings of the economy, they demanded a prompt response: "As soon as men resort to violence to bend others to their wills, all considerations but that of order must give way to the higher one of saving the country from anarchy." [62]

Having recoiled from the collective efforts of the rice workers as "violence to bend others to their wills," Porcher proceeded to describe an incident when his fellow white South Carolinians took matters into their own hands. An elderly white couple in Edgefield District were found murdered. Porcher wrote that suspicion against local black residents was soon "converted into certainty" by an alleged confession of guilt. Six men and two women were delivered to the sheriff. In the presence of a growing white mob, "some men disguised" approached the sheriff and blindfolded him. Next the prisoners, "all but the women," were led off into the nearby woods and executed. Porcher contended that neither the sheriff nor the local residents seemed to know who carried out the execution. "It would be unfair not to add," he continued, "that the public mind was not displeased that summary justice had speedily overtaken the perpetrators of the outrage upon the unhappy old couple." [63]

Porcher asked a lot to be believed that neither the sheriff nor anyone else seemed to know the vigilantes. His justification of the entire incident is similarly dubious, especially considering his indictment of the collective efforts of the rice workers. The execution of the African Americans suspected of murder, he wrote, was "an act of will-justice perpetrated by white men." Later he concluded, "When law is lax or impotent, society is forced to recur to first principles." The difference between "the unreasoning mob" who "resort to violence to bend others to their wills" and the act of "will-justice" to uphold order and save the nation from anarchy boiled down to which group performed the act.[64]

By the 1880s Porcher believed he had successfully reasserted important Old South values into a new, free-labor South Carolina. With his acceptance of certain laissez-faire principles, seeing economic forces operating as natural laws largely beyond human control, Porcher shed the planter class of blame for the defeat of the Old South. He remained focused on fundamental human inequalities and the personal leadership abilities of the traditional elite class. In a specific appeal to the "authority of history" he taught that white superiority was historically "true," that democracies were dangerous, and that elite rule was a bulwark of a civilized society, slave or free. All of these seemed consistent with the return of "Bourbon" political rule in 1877. In all, to a traditional conservative such as Porcher it must have seemed that South Carolina represented a sound, satisfying transition from a slave society to a free society. For people such as Edward McCrady Jr., however, one of Porcher's former students, the next fifteen years saw the surviving principles of the traditional southern conservatism come again under attack. This time criticism did not come from northern abolitionists or Union soldiers, but from fellow white South Carolinians.

CHAPTER THREE

The Public Business Is Ours

Edward McCrady Jr. and the Challenge from Below, 1865–1900

As did Frederick Porcher, one of his professors at the College of Charleston, Edward McCrady Jr. confirmed in his writings that beliefs in traditional elite rule and white supremacy, and the fears of majoritarian rule and political centralization, continued to shape conservative views. McCrady was an influential spokesman for the conservative resurgence in South Carolina in the 1870s. Highlighting the ever-changing world of the postwar South, however, McCrady in turn suffered politically for his conservative beliefs in the 1880s. By the end of the century a changing local economy coupled with persistent challenges from poorer white South Carolinians forced South Carolina conservatives to find new forms of expression for an old intellectual tradition.

Edward McCrady Jr. was born in Charleston in 1833. After graduating from the College of Charleston in 1853, McCrady was admitted to the bar in 1855, joining his prominent father, Edward McCrady Sr. The McCrady family owned land and slaves outside the city, reporting at least fifteen slaves for the 1860 census.[1] His city of birth, his family's position within society, and his education all served as rich sources of antebellum southern conservatism. McCrady was active in the state militia between 1854 and 1859, became a captain in the Meagher Guards, and was a member of one of the local companies that took Castle Pinckney in Charleston Harbor as tensions escalated in December 1860.[2] When the Civil War broke out, McCrady joined the First South Carolina Volunteers under Gen. Maxcy Gregg. McCrady saw extensive action from 1861 to 1863 and rose to lieutenant colonel by 1863. He was wounded severely at Second Manassas and again at Fredericksburg before being assigned command of an instructional camp in Madison, Florida, in 1864, which he finally surrendered in May 1865.[3]

Following the war McCrady returned to Charleston, where he resumed his law practice with his father. Long hours of study and work consumed his days and aggravated head and back wounds from the war, but his efforts garnered early success. Within the first year McCrady had a house on Meeting Street safely south of Broad Street—an important geographical distinction among Charleston's elite. The activities of McCrady's siblings and cousins show an elite family busily reestablishing itself in prominent positions. He reported in 1866 that his brother-in-law Thomas Bacot had retaken possession of family land from the Freedman's Bureau, although it was "very much injured as a place of residence." Despite the dire conditions of postwar Charleston, his brother John McCrady was made a full professor at the College of Charleston with an increase in pay. McCrady's cousin William Henry Trescot was in Washington, D.C., as "the agent of the state." [4] As the McCradys reorganized themselves socially and economically, they also helped the state's conservative faction regroup.

McCrady described "our people" in early 1866 as "quiet but anxious observers" of events in postwar Charleston, and he placed some hope that "the Lord seems to have raised up [Andrew] Johnson for some great purpose." By December 1866 uncertainty ruled the day, compounded by the knowledge that his fellow white Charlestonians "cannot influence it." McCrady counseled patience: "I think we have but one thing to do and that is to do nothing." [5] McCrady's fellow conservatives had certainly been active up to that point in time. They met in 1865 to rewrite the state's constitution, a version that included the infamous Black Codes restricting African American freedom in numerous ways. The state's representatives elected under the new constitution were then barred from taking their place in the national congress, signaling that local political struggles were far from over. Gen. Daniel Sickles, the military commander of South Carolina, declared the Black Codes invalid, and the state geared for another round of constitution writing, the result of which was the constitution of 1868. McCrady continued to advise a strategy of nonparticipation in 1870. A "press conference" of South Carolina's newspapers urged all citizens to recognize the right of suffrage, "irrespective of color" and as stipulated in the state's 1868 constitution. [6] The announcement also encouraged the organization of a movement for those "opposed to Radicalism and in favor of good and honest government." These "resolutions" gave McCrady an opportunity to assert into the postwar context traditional conservative principles. [7]

In a series of six articles McCrady argued that criticizing Republican Party rule while accepting black suffrage was dangerously inconsistent. McCrady was convinced that suffrage for the freedmen was not an end but rather a means of party control in the South. Therefore one could not accept black suffrage and still hope to reject party politics. South Carolina's conservatives should, he believed, withdraw from the political activities of the state. The answer lay "not in seeking office and meddling with the politics of our conquerors. Let education, agriculture, mechanics, and commerce be our only politics."[8] William Gilmore Simms, the influential conservative writer from antebellum days, concurred. "Let us hold ourselves aloof," Simms wrote McCrady, "touch not, handle not, taste not anything in common with our invaders; keep up communion among ourselves . . . in all the ancient circles." [9]

Charleston's conservatives did not confuse their message of separation with an attitude of surrender. Thomas M. Hanckel, writing in 1867, believed that the qualities engendered by slave owning would enable the traditional elite to survive these difficult years. Since the war, Hanckel wrote, they had "exhibited a kindly sympathy with their former dependents, an intelligent submission to necessity, an obedience to law and a regard for social order, combined with a firm self-respect, which have merited, we think, the approbation of all men." These attributes, he continued, harkening back to the days of slavery, were "the result of the habit of self-control, the daily sense of responsibility, the patient encounter with necessary evils, the carefulness for the welfare of their laborers, and the frequent interchange of acts of kindness, to all with which they were compelled by their Anglo-Saxon education, by the spirit of liberty and Christianity within them by the very necessities of their anomalous institution, and by its practical administration in the presence of Christendom."[10]

Hanckel's 1867 remarks were clearly directed toward a defense of racial hierarchy. He made a similar plea on behalf of hierarchy generally in 1859. Local rule, "within the limits of our sectional interests, our social sympathies, and our political fellowship," was for Hanckel "the most precious of all liberties." He highlighted the conservative South Carolinian's definition of liberty, with its clear emphasis on limits, by contrasting it with the Hungarian nationalist Lajos (Louis) Kossuth's definition. Hanckel chided Kossuth for trumpeting "the solidarity of human rights" as "the craziest notion that ever troubled the brain of a dreaming enthusiast or was coined into the phrases of a species rhetorician."[11]

Now in 1867 Hanckel continued to sound a note of warning. Not unlike Frederick Porcher's warnings against the rise of communism, Hanckel feared a time when the righteous would be called to unite against "the assaults of an infidel philosophy and a material humanitarianism." He reminded his readers that "the people of the South have always been ardently attached to the great principles of constitutional liberty, social order, and conservative law" and would remain so through their present trials. Hanckel thundered on, *"Fortuna non mutat genus."* Fortune did not change the "genus" of the conservative elite.[12]

Along the same lines, Charleston conservative Benjamin Huger Rutledge noted in an 1875 memorial service for the Confederate dead, "The antecedents of a people are the seeds of their after development."[13] Edward McCrady's advice to withdraw from politics might have appealed emotionally, but it served as poor strategy for elite white South Carolinians who knew intimately the connections between political, social, and economic power. As northern interest in Reconstruction waned, the opportunity arose to reinsert themselves into the bitter, often bloody, political contests of the state. This effort succeeded in 1876 with the election as governor of Wade Hampton, a Democrat, former Confederate general, and one of the Old South's largest slaveholders.

The campaign of 1876 shows that McCrady abruptly abandoned his earlier plans to "do nothing" politically. He was the leader of the Sumter Guards, one of the many local "rifle clubs" that intimidated the African American majority under the guise of enforcing social order.[14] When Reconstruction governor Daniel Chamberlain attempted to disband the rifle clubs in 1876, McCrady wrote his cousin Edward McCrady L'Engle, "We have determined to stand by our arms." Their weaponry included several field artillery pieces that McCrady was preparing to place on a boat to Florida so as to prevent them from "falling into the hands of the enemy." His defiance knew its limits, however. "Of course if the U.S. Govt interferes," he explained, they would "not be so foolish" as to challenge federal soldiers.[15]

With Wade Hampton's victory in 1876–77, McCrady and fellow conservatives once again spoke as a ruling political elite. In his victory address Hampton referred to himself as the "representative of the conservative party."[16] Through articles and speeches they put forward a reinvigorated vision of a hierarchical conservative regime.[17] The regime was to be maintained with few apologies by limited political participation through race and class discrimination and, if necessary, violence against dissent.[18] Fraud, violence, intimidation, "all these good, bad and indifferent," McCrady granted, were means of regaining political control; but then he asked, "For what? To leave it as we found it?"[19] As historian E. Culpepper Clark has noted, conservatives worried that the recurring violence surrounding the state's elections contained "the chaotic seeds of their own undoing," but by 1880 conservatives such as McCrady who had accepted the violence of 1876 now offered themselves as the "harbingers of moderation, stability, and order." [20]

McCrady was not alone in sensing that a golden opportunity had arrived for the state's traditional elite. In 1877 Belton O'Neall Townsend, writing as "A South Carolinian," published three essays in *Atlantic Monthly* dissecting the state of affairs in South Carolina. While much of Townsend's analysis was critical of the traditional elite, he offered impressive insight into the persisting influence the elite had even after the war. He noted that despite the dramatically changed circumstances from those of the Old South, "At this day, as of old, Southern aristocrats are our public men and statesmen." While the elite class's financial strength was not what it once was, "their ancestral distinction and their intelligence and social superiority to the mass of the whites have remained intact." Townsend's account continues with an air of disbelief: "Gentlemen of the old school abound among us, can be told from all others by their indescribable air of cultivation and distinction, and are worshiped by the people." He added: "Whenever an aristocrat is compelled to mingle with the respectable and working classes, they treat him with a respect which is positively amazing; there is a tacit understanding on both sides that he is among them but not of them. . . . their political ascendency is yet looked on, and will long be looked on by the Southern whites as an unquestionable portion of the eternal fitness of things." Certainly this is what men such as Edward McCrady Jr. and Frederick Porcher believed of themselves and their cohort. It appeared now in 1877 that the world had been set right, or close to it, once again.[21]

Setting the conservative tone for constitutional reform, Theodore G. Barker, another Charlestonian, placed the traditionally antidemocratic views of South Carolina's ruling elite within growing national doubts about majoritarian rule. Addressing the Washington Artillery Club in 1876, Barker observed that Americans, "without regard to section or State," were beginning to question "how far an unchecked and aggressive spirit of Democracy, as expressed, for instance, in universal suffrage or in the cry of the divine right of the mere majority, is the boon now."[22] Barker's disgust for the American faith in majority rule predated the Civil War. In a raucous speech on behalf of South Carolina's drive toward secession, Barker sneered at the North: "See their forms of Democracy driving onward to the licence of mob-law, and their conservatism quailing before the tyranny of mere numbers."[23] Barker in 1876 worried that the modern era lacked "the unexampled conservatism, which pervaded the political and social life of the last century; a conservatism which led the people to choose as their natural and proper representatives as Washington, Hamilton, and Madison." Barker held that the

Founding Fathers' conservatism wisely surrounded "new political machinery . . . with the wisest safeguards that political wisdom has ever invented; not to perpetuate their own power, but to protect the people, whom they had successfully led, and who were ready almost to crown them for their work."[24] Too much democracy tore away at the "safeguards" surrounding government and, Barker could have added, jeopardized elites' ability to maintain their control over a changing South Carolina society.

Conservative fears of an uneducated electorate, black or white, with unobstructed access to the political process flourished in 1876–77. The strong conservative themes Barker found in the story of national independence—a story of "natural and proper representatives" chosen to "protect the people"—resonated among McCrady's friends in the mid-1870s. In an 1876 address to the South Carolina Historical Society, of which McCrady was a devoted member and later president, the historian William J. Rivers worried that the "republican form of government . . . has come to mean . . . nothing else than a numerical majority, with suffrage by every man without regard to race, color, previous condition of servitude, property, or education" and added that "so cheap and indiscriminate has become this right of citizenship that even women are claiming participation in it."[25] John Julius Pringle Smith in 1877 made the observation that "constitutional limitations become irksome when they obstruct the will of a majority"; he continued that when respect for those limitations ceased in a simple democracy, "then that will becomes a 'vulgar tyranny.'" It was against this, Smith claimed, that the leaders of "restoration" acted, and he lauded them as those who "alone have the right to dictate how South Carolina shall be governed."[26]

As one of those claiming the right to "dictate," McCrady perceived a problem in the state's 1868 constitution. Well aware of the formidable political presence African Americans represented in South Carolina, McCrady admitted that whites would likely resort to violence against black voters to keep them from the polls or engage in fraud within the existing political system. McCrady did not hesitate to say that of the two, "by all means let us hazard violence . . . rather than resort to fraud. Violence will not degrade us, as fraud will." Violence, he reasoned, implied an opponent, an enemy. Fraud "will be a calamity inflicted not by others, but by ourselves. We will be degraded by our own act."[27]

Rather than either of these options, McCrady sought other ways of limiting access to the political process. The "necessities of revolution" justified the means of regaining political power, but, he now concluded, government could not continue in a constant state of revolution. He argued that it was time to lay out "honestly and manfully" a continuing problem within the white elite position. White political leaders, he asserted, still operated under the theory that "white people—that is, the people who have all the intelligence, and all the property," would act as a unit. McCrady rejected this. The notion worked during a crisis, he conceded, but whites being whites, i.e., intelligent, it could not be expected that "one who thinks for himself will long subordinate his conviction to others." Therefore the dreadful specter of whites competing with whites for the black vote remained, since McCrady assumed African Americans would always act as a "race." "Negroes can be kept together," he explained, "because they are ignorant." McCrady cautioned his fellow white South Carolinians, "Let us not deceive ourselves—just as sure as that vote remains as it is . . . it will be used."[28]

McCrady expressed his racism in his post-Reconstruction articles through the general theme of the unfortunate ignorance of African Americans, rather than their innate barbarism or their "falling back towards . . . heathens and savages," as he had described them in 1870. But behind what appear to be racist platitudes lie the South Carolina conservative outlook on class as well. By presenting African Americans' unfitness for political participation as a matter of intelligence, McCrady established a standard of the necessary, fundamental qualities for self-government that he in turn applied to poorer and likewise uneducated whites. A year before his 1880 election to the state house of representatives from Charleston, McCrady stated that the most honest way to achieve good government was to establish suffrage qualifications through literacy requirements. These standards would be "applicable alike to black and white" and would "elevate the standard of citizenship of all so as to insure an intelligent participation."[29]

As a state congressman, McCrady in 1880 introduced legislation along these very lines. McCrady's Eight-Box Law stipulated that a voter needed to be able to read the names of the candidates and offices in order to place the ballots in the corresponding ballot boxes.[30] Proposal of the bill prompted outrage that perhaps thousands of white South Carolinians would be disfranchised by literacy requirements. The *News and Courier,* normally a staunch conservative organ, worried openly: "We doubt that half the white voters in the State would be able to place all eight ballots in the proper boxes."[31] Writing on behalf of poorer, illiterate whites and tearing at the notion of racial unity even in the state's past, "B." wrote to the Charleston paper that "it is too often that a certain class of leaders are indignant when their views are opposed" and continued in ominous terms: "To require a man, a free man, a white man, one who followed (contrary to his better convictions) his leaders in the late war and fought the whole four years' term, with all its sacrifices, to be compelled to pay for the privilege of voting will be the crushing straw that broke the camel's back. . . . If you pass the bill as introduced it will act as a cleaver that will divide the Democratic party in South Carolina to the four winds and then if Mahoneism steps in and usurps the power I guess you will understand who was to blame."[32]

McCrady remained undaunted, stating that "if the public good requires, we must not shrink from the enforcement of the rule even on their account." He understood clearly that his law would result in white disfranchisement, saying, "we care not if it does. . . . To them, too, we say the schools are open." McCrady hoped that the bill would force the "indolent" to educate themselves into informed citizens. In what must have seemed typical lowcountry fashion, and what was typical southern conservative fashion, McCrady assumed that he and his fellows spoke for what the "public good requires" and that thus "*we*" must not shrink from action "even on *their* account."[33]

Fellow conservatives William Porcher Miles and Thomas Hanckel agreed with McCrady that a literate electorate offered the political stability that, in their eyes, the South Carolina democracy lacked. Miles, president of the reorganized South Carolina College, observed, "If Republican government, based upon universal suffrage, be not destined, after proving a farce, to become a tragedy, the whole people must be educated." Miles made clear that his fellow conservatives "do not wish to see the colored man deprived of the right of suffrage because he is a colored man." Rather, Miles echoed McCrady's view: "I speak for myself and many, at least, of the best men of the State, who are conservative enough to believe, and bold enough to avow, that universal, unqualified suffrage is an evil when exercised by the entire adult population of any race or any color" (years later H. R. Ravenel weighed in that "perhaps when the negroes have learned enough . . . they will have become more conservative voters").[34]

Hanckel, an alumnus of South Carolina College from the antebellum days, saw the literacy requirements as both a source of stability for the state and an opportunity for the already educated, conservative elite. Arguing that "society is organized by ideas, and governments are ruled by thought," Hanckel implored his fellow South Carolina College alumni, "We must control the one if we hope to possess and direct the other"; he added, "Let me teach your people and I will soon write their statutes. Let me govern your scholars and

I will soon govern your State."[35] This was an idea no doubt shared by Frederick Porcher at the College of Charleston.

In an 1880 address McCrady continued to flesh out his thesis of literacy and education as "the very basis of our political organization."[36] He began by noting that the United States and South Carolina were governed by written constitutions. As was shown with Frederick Porcher, this was not an inconsequential point. From Burke to Calhoun and through the late 1800s, conservatives debated the merits and weaknesses of the written constitutions. Nineteenth-century conservatives viewed written constitutions, particularly the U.S. Constitution, as lacking historical legitimacy and susceptible to manipulation—"mere parchment," Porcher called the constitution in 1831.[37] In the context of South Carolina in 1880, McCrady hoped to turn the undeniable fact of governance through a written constitution to conservative advantage through his plan for literacy requirements. Simply put, a country governed, for better or worse, by a written constitution should be governed by a people who could read the document.

Making use of an extensive body of British literature in the nineteenth century that critiqued the merits and dangers of democracy, McCrady utilized the arguments of fellow politician and historian Thomas Macaulay to justify disfranchisement. Opposing the "People's Charter," Macaulay in 1842 conceded that it was not entirely the fault of the poor and ignorant that they were in fact poor and ignorant and that a better educational system would have alleviated some of the problems. "But," McCrady quoted Macaulay, "is that a reason for giving them the franchise, when their own position proves that they are not fit for it; when they give us fair notice that if we let them have it, they will use it for our own ruin and their own?" McCrady concurred heartily with this reasoning: "Unfortunately, alike for the whites and blacks of the South, no such words of wisdom and of justice were uttered, or listened to, if uttered in the Halls of Congress, when the Reconstruction measures were proposed." Becoming at least marginally more sensitive to the politics of white disfranchisement, McCrady at one point employed a Lost Cause theme, reaching for, if not believing in, a vision of an organic, white southern society. The disfranchisement of some whites may occur, "however much we might regret the necessity." But, added former Confederate colonel Edward McCrady of Maxcy Gregg's Brigade, surely this was not too much to ask of a people who sacrificed twelve thousand men in the recent war; "brave men," he was sure, who "would submit even to this sacrifice, if necessary for the good of the State for which they freely offered their very lives." Evidently it was, however.[38]

During the antebellum years the institution of slavery held together well enough the conservatives' simultaneous beliefs in white rule over black South Carolinians and in elite rule over all. In a free South Carolina the twin pillars of race *and* class rule stood on an inherently unstable foundation. Older notions of one's place frequently failed to address a changing economy and a new constitutional order. Black South Carolinians were not slaves. With the rise of the textile mills, poor whites were not bound to lives of hardscrabble farming and later tenantry. Postwar conservatives, therefore, were constantly being forced to aim their salvos in defense of hierarchy at moving targets.

Assessing the state's political situation in 1880, McCrady's thoughts revealed the shifting foundations underneath the postwar hierarchies of race and class. He first noted that white South Carolinians "have not only to study and to practice how to govern ourselves, but how to do so with an inferior race forced upon us as our equals." South Carolina's black population meanwhile continued to receive educational support from northern missionary groups that McCrady believed were "lavishing upon the negro means of education which are wanting to the whites." He worried lest "the negroes of the South . . . should at least for the while, be better educated than the masses of the whites." If present trends continued and enough black voters met the educational qualification to vote, whites would again face "black rule."[39]

McCrady never questioned his belief in whites' intellectual superiority. But he also did not relish having to endure too much confusion on the matter. Under the Eight-Box Bill, African American voters only had to become "better educated" than poor whites, and evidence that this was happening clearly unsettled McCrady. Literacy qualifications satisfied his conservative desire to check the unwieldy forces of mass democracy. But the prospect of massive white disfranchisement and the rise of qualified, black political control undermined in a very public way the conservative belief in white supremacy. Moreover, as the letter from "B." to the *News and Courier* made perfectly clear, the bill threatened McCrady's and the conservative regime's political standing within South Carolina. In the end, the election law of 1882 gave wide latitude to local election managers to determine who had successfully placed their ballots in the correct boxes and who had not. Not surprisingly, thousands of African American voters were disfranchised in the process.

After Reconstruction, Hampton, McCrady, and the rest of the "Bourbon" leadership fought to contain a number of restless movements within the state. The hard-line racist movement led by former Confederate general Martin W. Gary of Edgefield emerged on the heels of "restoration" itself. Gary and his followers remained incensed even by the limited extent to which the Hampton administration was willing to consider black voters' concerns at the seeming expense of their pressing needs. The *Yorkville Enquirer* worried in 1878 that the "majority of the laboring class of the country are today without one month's rations on hand."[40] Martin Gary complained meanwhile, "I suppose we shall next hear of '*dining*' or *dancing* with the colored brothers and sisters as events the natural result of Hampton Democracy."[41] A meeting of African American political leaders gathered in 1883 to protest the practical results of the new election law, namely their disfranchisement. It was, they proclaimed, "the most damnable form of State Government to which a free people have ever been subjected."[42] In the mid-1880s the Knights of Labor attempted to recruit both African American and white farm workers.[43] None of these stirrings of protest, however, matched the intensity or reach of Benjamin R. Tillman's "farmers" movement beginning in 1886.

The rise of "Pitchfork" Ben Tillman in the 1880s has been treated by skilled historians such as Francis B. Simkins, William J. Cooper Jr., and more recently Stephen Kantrowitz.[44] Ben Tillman rose to the head of a Democratic faction that, while not made up exclusively of poor farmers—Tillman himself was not poor—was certainly in its tone and rhetoric antiaristocratic. Initially motivated by hard-times farming in the early 1880s, Tillman and his followers by the late 1880s had moved on to engage the traditional conservatives in a high-stakes debate over a wide range of issues, including the future educational system of the state, race relations, the state's relationship with the federal government, and even the meaning of South Carolina's history.[45]

Through the same years that Frederick Porcher was developing his sense of laissez-faire conservatism, Tillman and his followers, while not aligned with the Populist Party, shared some of the concerns that drove the Populists in the South and the Midwest, as well as the labor movement in the North. Farmers and laborers increasingly shared the view that they had been made to endure economic difficulties through little fault of their own. They grew frustrated by a society and a system of government that seemed run by and for the elite—whether they were the industrial elite of the North or "Charleston's rich politicians" in South Carolina.[46] Having not attended the lectures on laissez-faire governance taught by conservatives such as Porcher, South Carolina's farmers clearly envisioned a role to be played by the state in connection with their economic well-being. They had, it may be presumed, been taught the glories of representative government, and they were, after all, citizens. Their determination to have the government work on their behalf and through their vote was logical and forceful.

In 1890 the Farmers Association, the official name for the Tillman movement, published what became referred to as the Shell Manifesto, a full-scale assault on South Carolina's ruling elite. The Tillmanite "reformers" stated their differences from the traditional conservatives in the first sentence. Contrasting itself sharply from the conservative paeans to rule by an elite few and for "the general good," the manifesto, written by Tillman, established its plan to work through the Democratic Party toward a "recognition of the needs and rights of the masses." Ben Tillman's association claimed credit as "Inch by Inch and step by step true Democracy—the rule *of* the people—has won its way." The state's traditional rulers, on the other hand, "those who have been and are still governing our State," were cast as "enemies of true Jeffersonian democracy." [47]

Tillman's association also offered its followers an alternative reading of South Carolina history. From seventeenth-century rule by the Lords Proprietors of Carolina on, there existed "an aristocracy under the forms of Democracy." Tillman gave his own history lesson, hammering at the state's traditional elite and openly appealing to "the people": "Whenever a champion of the people has attempted to show them their rights . . . an aristocratic oligarchy has bought him with an office, or . . . turned loose the floodgates of misrepresentation and slander." The Tillman movement used its view of the past to take a clearly directed shot at the conservative regime and antebellum southern conservatism: "Can we afford to leave it [the state] longer in the hands of those wedded to ante-bellum ideas, but possessing little of antebellum patriotism and honor?" In what must have seemed confirmation of conservatives' worst fears, the Shell Manifesto, borrowing words from a rather notorious opponent of southern conservatives, called upon "every true Carolinian, of all classes and calling" to "give us a government of the people, by the people, and for the people." [48]

For decades before and after the war southern conservatives raised a loud howl about northern aggression against their "existing institutions." Indeed much of their defense of slavery as revealed truth through time and their subsequent attack on Reconstruction was founded on this premise. The Tillmanites had little time for such notions: "All the cry about 'existing institutions' which must remain inviolate," Tillman claimed, merely masked conservatives' plans "in the future, as in the past, to get all they can, and keep all they get." In this one blunt sentence Tillman struck effectively at the many and often elaborate conservative pretensions about their own leadership being "for the general good." The Tillman movement countered this with a candid admission that reflected the spread of mass democracy through the 1800s: "If we control the State Democratic Convention, a Legislature in sympathy will naturally follow." [49]

The openness by which South Carolina's conservatives such as McCrady expressed their views of society, government, and their elevated place within each added fuel to Tillman's fire. In an 1887 commencement address given at The Citadel, McCrady presented a thinly veiled caricature of Tillman and his followers. Urging the graduates to participate politically, McCrady pointed out that by "politics" he did not mean "the seeking and scheming for office . . . the truckling and fauning for votes . . . the anxious watch to catch the first shiftings of popular opinion . . . the art of personal popularity without regard to the welfare of the State." McCrady's criticism of the modern politician segued into the conservative criticism of democracy. The modern politician was "stirring and striving." In the degrading effort to attain "civil greatness" the democratic politician sacrificed principle. The modern politician was "one always on the watch for the coming reaction . . . one who has no faith in doctrine, no zeal for any cause." Much as Porcher had explained in his comparisons of republics and democracies, the newer, more democratic politician was one "who sneers . . . at those who are anxious to preserve." There was, he added, "nothing in the State which he could not without a scruple or blush join in defending or destroying."[50]

Even while the Tillman movement gained momentum, McCrady speculated that there still might be a place for his kind of politician and politics. He first took his audience through a brief lesson on the nature of governments and the possibilities for conservative rule within the "numerous democracy" that South Carolina was apparently becoming. As students, he noted, they had been taught that there were three kinds of governments: "the government of one—the monarchy; the government of a few—an oligarchy; or the government of all—a democracy." Happily he noted that "the tendency of the first and last of these is, each to the second." A monarch needed advisers, and often in lieu of a competent monarch the advisers in fact ruled. In a democracy "what is every body's business, is apt to be nobody's business," and therefore "we generally leave the rule to a few, whose personal interest make it their business to attend to public affairs." These were not bad tendencies in all, and the benefits when the right people were "the few" who actually ruled could be shown through American history. McCrady referred to another noted conservative, John Adams, who in 1814 wrote approvingly of "aristocratical caucuses" in churches, towns, and counties that served to assist "all this complication of machinery" that accompanied general elections. The difference to McCrady between a primary, a caucus, and a convention—a point of contention between Tillman's people and the conservatives—was not the issue. His point was that conservative forces take note of the potential for elite rule within all three.[51]

McCrady used the conservative bastion before him, the Citadel, to hammer home his point on the political responsibilities of the elite: "The State had no right to select you . . . for your own individual advantage. It must act with a single eye and purpose to the general good—the good of all." Just as the state had the right to punish for the public good, so too should education be "only for the welfare of the community." For the select few at the Citadel, the state "has educated you that you should be the better citizens." The wording here was clearly no accident; as soon-to-be members of a ruling elite they were not simply better citizens but "the better citizens." Applying the same logic to politics, he stated bluntly the conservative presumption to rule, proclaiming to the next generation of leadership that "under our system of government, the public business is ours—just as much ours as our own personal and private affairs."[52]

A few months prior to his Citadel address in 1887 McCrady suffered the indignity of having a letter published by a disgruntled client, a Dr. T. C. Robertson, denouncing him as "guilty of falsehood, treachery, and scoundrelism" over a questionable mortgage transfer. The letter acknowledged the likelihood of legal action in response to its contents and concluded that such an action, even if successful, would associate his name "with all that is dishonorable." The letter did indeed bring a response from McCrady, who sued Robertson for libel. The case came before the court of common pleas in April 1888 and was decided in McCrady's favor. The opening statements by his attorney Charles Richardson Miles set the tone for plaintiff McCrady and reminded those in the courtroom of the powerful conservative tradition still alive in South Carolina. Miles noted, "We live in what is doubtless in many respects a 'new South' and a new 'South Carolina,' and many 'old things have passed away,'" but, he added pointedly, "amid new institutions and new standards of life and conduct the traditions and sentiments and prejudices of our old social life are still potent factors." This invocation of the conservative tradition succeeded. The jury found Robertson guilty of libel and awarded McCrady twenty-five hundred dollars of the ten thousand dollars sought.[53]

Letters of congratulations to McCrady reveal that the case had taken on symbolic importance for conservative South Carolinians. What appear to be standard plaudits for the victor have a more pointed meaning given the political and social tensions between conservatives and their dissenters in the Tillman movement. One writer, J. Middleton, assured McCrady that he had "the sympathy of all thinking men" and hoped that the verdict would "do a great deal towards purifying the moral atmosphere." Robert Aldrich of Barnwell was likewise pleased, "knowing the prejudice which the average jurymen entertain towards a gentleman." Julius Heyward wrote from Greenville that his concern was never with McCrady but rather for "the singularly weak jury, composed of shop-keepers and 'sand-hillers.'" The praise reached a crescendo in a letter from John D. Edwards, who hoped that the public recognition of McCrady's "truth, moral courage, high tone, and christian forbearance" signaled "the dawn of a higher plane, a higher tone to the society of this state, and one which our higher civilization demands." Edwards believed McCrady's victory to be "the stepping stone to that new system in South Carolina which will constitute the bulwarks of society, and make moral courage the standard of right instead of brute force and foul words."[54]

McCrady shared in this brief season of conservative optimism. In a speech given the same year as his libel trial, he cited British historian William E. H. Lecky's *England in the Eighteenth Century* and its discussion of England's rule by the Romans and later the Normans. McCrady wondered aloud: "Conquered England absorbed and changed and moulded her conquerors. Will this be our case?"[55] But such optimism proved short-lived. By 1890, just three years after McCrady's proud assertion to the graduates of the Citadel that "the public business is *ours,*" Ben Tillman was back on the political scene stronger than ever. The man who had previously called for the abolition of the Citadel, what he called "that military dude factory," decided that the farmers of the state needed more than just a Tillman movement; they needed Tillman as governor.[56]

The change in tone between 1887 and 1890 in McCrady's writings and the letters he received reflected the jolt South Carolina's conservatives received by Tillman's resurgence. Before the election the *News and Courier* published under the revealing title "Our Danger and Our Duty" an interview with McCrady. McCrady wavered on how serious the divisions were among white South Carolinians. His personal hatred of Tillman prompted him to dismiss the renegade: "Politically he is only a symptom—a symptom of discontent. Kill him off and unless you find and remove the cause of unrest some one else will take his place." When asked about the cause of discontent, however, McCrady downplayed the extent of dissent and suggested that the trouble was one of perception. South Carolinians were upset because they believed that the state's primary elections were still not being run cleanly. McCrady chalked up the dissent to "mistake or exaggeration" but then granted that there was "no doubt of some real cause for complaint."[57]

McCrady's uncertain handling of the Tillman movement was not uncommon for South Carolina's conservatives. The response of a Columbia lawyer to Tillman's attack on General Hampton sums up the conservative disbelief and then rage: "In the very presence of Hampton, I have heard this man strike with poisoned tongue at the vitals of our civilization. It is incumbent upon us to take this man by the throat and choke him until his lips are livid and until he retracts his infamous insinuations."[58]

McCrady received other letters that underscored the sense of shock at the persistent and very personal protest from within white South Carolina. As Tillman's election as governor grew likely, conservatives feverishly reassessed their tactics. This intense conservative self-analysis spread the blame around. G. W. Gage wrote to McCrady blaming the *News and Courier:* "With stupid persistency, it is driving the people of the State to a support of Tillman, by ridicule and misrepresentation."[59] Another correspondent, J. M. B. Reeves, opted to shorten the internal lines of defense within conservative ranks to the Charleston area: "It were well for Charleston if the Democratic party as at present constituted, could be 'disrupted.' . . . We want independence in local [i.e., Charleston] matters."[60] Sen. Matthew C. Butler, acknowledging Tillman's imminent election, wrote that "Tillman could have been beaten by vigorous and thorough organization of the opposing elements," and echoing McCrady's complaint of the modern politician, Butler continued: "Office seekers have climbed on the backs of the farmers, the most gullible element in all communities, to ride into office and from present appearances they will succeed."[61] Later Butler wrote that he would try and reach some arrangement with the Tillmanites but confessed, "I hav'nt [*sic*] much faith in the venture."[62]

The Shell Manifesto and the Tillman campaign, as William Cooper put it, "exploded the deceptive political calm."[63] South Carolina's traditional elite organized late to combat the Tillman campaign and lost badly at the state convention in September. Alexander Haskell's campaign as a "Conservative" independent candidate fared poorly as well. Butler's lack of enthusiasm was warranted; as historian Francis B. Simkins summarized it succinctly but accurately, "It was too late."[64]

McCrady spent the 1890s generating some renown as the state's preeminent historian. Lacking political position and reflecting the conservative faith in the past as a source of time-tested values and institutions, McCrady through his historical work set forth the principles and qualities he felt South Carolina and the nation were recklessly abandoning. The line between the more explicitly political writings and those of a historical nature was never completely drawn, nor by the logic of nineteenth-century conservative thought should it be drawn. Therefore his "political" speeches frequently had ample historical references and his "historical" works contained clear political lessons.

As a historian McCrady often turned to colonial South Carolina as a convenient source for the wisdom of conservative thought. For example, in 1897 he presented a paper to the Society of Colonial Dames that could be read as a prospectus for his four-volume history of South Carolina that ends in 1783. Explaining the settlement of South Carolina, McCrady relished the chance to criticize the fancy notions of the "great philosopher" John Locke. Conservatives had long lambasted Locke for his Enlightenment views on equality and natural rights. But in the context of South Carolina history, the "great philosopher" himself drew up the "Fundamental Constitutions" that governed the proprietary colony in the early 1700s. McCrady argued that the imposition of a constructed, experimental governmental system over the American colonists was folly: "The whole scheme was visionary, crude, incomplete, impractical and ridiculous." The point is not too subtle. Society finds its own, best form of government over time and naturally. South Carolina's traditional, local elites were tried and tested through the state's own history and found worthy of leadership. The "grand fundamental constitutions" had failed and proved "the absurdity of the grand model of government."[65]

McCrady's increasing interest in historical work—for instance his massive four-volume history of South Carolina and his presidency of the South Carolina Historical Society—followed proportionately the decreasing political strength of conservatives through the 1890s. Once in power Tillman's forces dealt conservatives a further blow by choosing not to send Gen. Wade Hampton, the symbolic leader connecting the Old South to the postwar era and the hero of "restoration," back to the United States Senate. Ben Tillman won reelection in 1892 by an even wider margin than in 1890. In 1894 Tillman moved on to a seat in the United States Senate. Also in 1894 the Tillman forces called for statewide elections to a constitutional convention. The issue was clear: Tillman intended to rewrite the state constitution to eliminate further the black vote. McCrady and Hampton both urged their fellow conservatives to organize against the convention. They were badly outnumbered, however, and the constitutional convention of 1895 met with 112 Tillmanites, 42 Conservatives, and 6 Republicans (all of whom were African American). The convention debates resembled earlier debates over suffrage qualifications. The lines were not drawn strictly between Tillmanites and the Conservatives and Republicans. Charleston conservative John Pendleton Kennedy Bryan helped the Tillman delegates craft the disfranchising language.[66]

Still, constitutional reform aimed at removing a particular group of voters was tricky business. African American delegates pointed out eloquently the hypocrisy of disfranchising black voters while leaving poor whites on voting lists. Thomas E. Miller argued before the white delegates that "this country and its institutions are as much the common birthright and heritage of the American negro as it is the possession of you and yours. We have fought in every Indian war, in every foreign war, in every domestic struggle by the side of white soldiers from Boston commons and Lake Erie to the Mississippi valley and the banks of the Rio Grande." The *Sumter Watchman and Southron* went so far as to claim that the black delegates "have had altogether the best of the argument . . . and there is no dignified way out of the dilemma into which the majority of the convention has been forced," suggesting a solution along conservative lines: "An educational and property qualification will solve the problem of suffrage in South Carolina by eliminating the votes of the ignorant and irresponsible of both races."[67] Since dignity never came easily to Pitchfork Ben Tillman, his forces carried the day anyway. Through a battery of registration requirements and especially the loophole of an understanding clause, the 1895 constitution nearly eliminated the black vote in South Carolina.[68]

By 1899 McCrady had grown weary and wary of constitutions. When his niece Louisa Rebecca Barnwell wrote in 1899 asking for advice in studying the U.S. Constitution, McCrady growled in reply, "If you want to know the constitution of the U.S. at present you need not hear lectures. It can be written in one word 'force'"; he continued, "It was 'force' in our war against the most solemn engagements any people ever entered into . . . and its [*sic*] going to be *force* against all patience of constitutional law."[69] Conservatives such as McCrady likened the political defeats of the 1890s to the military defeat of 1865. The prevailing southern view of the war held that the Confederacy fell to superior Yankee resources and population. In the new, modern democracy South Carolina's conservatives learned over and over again that numbers mattered.

As the century drew to a close in 1898 McCrady received a letter from his cousin William Henry Trescot, the venerable South Carolina politician, diplomat, and scholar whose fame had peaked in the antebellum era. "I confess I am looking in intent wonder at the condition of the State," Trescot wrote; "what and where is the Conservative party in the State?"[70] Trescot's wonderment was valid. Events in the 1890s seem to support historian William J. Cooper's conclusion that the political defeat of the Conservatives by Tillman in 1890 was "as final as that of 1865."[71] Yet the question McCrady raised in 1888 about whether or not his fellow conservatives would be able to "absorb" and "change" and "mould" their "conquerors" remained open.[72] McCrady's question echoes William J. Rivers's encouragement in 1876 to the conservative survivors of the Old South to "infuse her nature" into the new era.[73]

As the century closed, younger South Carolina conservatives began waging a successful battle in other areas and through other means. Even before the century closed, the evidence was encouraging. Tillman biographers Francis B. Simkins and Stephen Kantrowitz both noted that Tillman's love of democracy had clear limits. Simkins argued that Tillman grew more conservative after the turn of the century, while Kantrowitz asserted that a self-centered, power-hungry Tillman had never really been interested in building a broadbased democratic movement.[74] Thus events of the 1890s challenged severely the conservative ability to maintain political and economic dominance. But these same years also offered new opportunities for power and new outlets for influence and ideas.

CHAPTER FOUR

Nearly Hopeless of Ever Elevating Either Negroes or Crackers

Theodore Jervey Jr. and the New Century

Wade Hampton, the postwar symbol of South Carolina conservatism, died in 1902. Gone also were other conservative stalwarts with direct ties to the Old South: Edward McCrady Jr., William Henry Trescot, and Matthew C. Butler all died around the turn of the century. For individuals such as Theodore Jervey, Jr. and William Watts Ball, born and reared in the southern conservative tradition, the decades surrounding the new century were perplexing. Woodrow Wilson, a contemporary, admitted as much in 1909, confessing, "We have stumbled upon a confusing age; nothing is like it was fifteen years ago."[1] During those years South Carolina disfranchised its black voters and created a series of Jim Crow laws. All South Carolinians observed with wonder the arrival of modern amenities such as the telephone, electric lights, and electric streetcars. Perhaps the biggest change of all, nearly fifty thousand South Carolinians worked in textile mills by 1910. The state's textile production rose dramatically to compete with Massachusetts for national leadership, and a new kind of person appeared on the scene, the millworker (dubbed immediately a "problem" by the state's traditional elite). Like Woodrow Wilson, Jervey and Ball responded by aligning themselves for a time with the new southern progressivism that sought, in Dewey Grantham's words, a "reconciliation of progress and tradition."[2] If William Henry Trescot could not find his conservatism in South Carolina, as he wrote to Edward McCrady Jr. in 1897, he would have been well advised to examine the emerging progressive movement, had he lived. With similar emphases on good governance, racial hierarchy, and rule by "the best" in society, the southern conservative tradition provided a valuable foundation for a newer, "progressive" spirit of the early 1900s. Old South conservatives would have likely appreciated the progressives' belief in the power of "institutions" to support elite rule and to care for the ever-present poor and ignorant.

Despite their stunning political defeats of 1890, South Carolina's conservatives persisted in their attacks on the state's democratic impulses. Even while political success in the state for a time went to those who reveled in antielite rhetoric, elite South Carolinians were developing other means of sending conservative messages. For example, conservatives continued to make effective use of the old general Wade Hampton. John A. Rice, writing in the 1940s, still thrilled to the image presented by Wade Hampton. Rice recalled being in complete awe seeing Hampton as an old man riding his horse through the streets of Columbia. "I wanted deep down in me to be like Wade Hampton," Rice wrote. Hampton, Rice noted, was beloved by "ordinary folks" as "sometimes general, sometimes governor, sometimes senator, always hero." Rice went on, however, to clarify that to South Carolina's conservatives, Hampton's "heroism" meant something slightly different. To postwar conservatives looking for a hero, "Wade Hampton was the perfect example." Hampton had "first . . . fought the Yankees and lost; then he had fought the poor whites and lost." As a result, Rice concluded, "he was a great man."[3]

As Confederate reunions and rituals flourished in the 1890s, South Carolina's traditional conservatives seized on the opportunity to promote their core values. Confederate reunions in South Carolina, and especially in Charleston, in the 1890s had a peculiar way of turning into celebrations for Wade Hampton. Celebrations for Wade Hampton had a peculiar way of turning into celebrations of conservative values. The *News and Courier* certainly did its part to interpret the Hampton Days as conservative, more than Confederate, celebrations. In the 1895 celebration Theodore G. Barker made yet another timely appearance on behalf of the conservative cause, introducing Hampton before a packed audience at Charleston's Academy of Music. Running through Hampton's war exploits, Barker carried his introduction through Hampton's postwar, post-Reconstruction career as well. Capturing the sense of outrage and disappointment at Tillman's election in 1890 and Tillman's refusal to send Hampton back to the U.S. Senate, Barker capped his introduction of Hampton as "the stone which the political builders of 1890 refused." The next day's press coverage continued the conservative themes behind what ostensibly was a joint meeting of the Sons of Confederate Veterans and United Daughters of the Confederacy. The newspaper also ran a statement written by the "Women of Carolina," who wrote how "the Greeks banished Aristides, poisoned Socrates, degraded Epaminondas" and in 1890 "the mob of South Carolina put aside Wade Hampton."[4]

The symbolism and pageantry of Wade Hampton Days in 1891, 1895, and 1898 resembled the royal ceremonies described in Arno Mayer's *The Persistence of the Old Regime: Europe to the Great War.* Mayer claims that pageants and celebrations featuring the European monarchies of the late nineteenth century represented "ceremonial rearticulation of calibrated cohesion in the upper class" and that all, "high and low," were to be "awed rather than cowed" by the majesty accompanying the public presentation of their traditional rulers.[5] The *News and Courier* re-created the stir generated by Hampton's appearance at the evening session of the 1898 Confederate reunion in Charleston: "As the old hero entered the hall every man and woman in it got up on a chair, sent up a cheer that might have been heard on Fort Sumter on a still night. Then the band came down with 'Dixie,' with a crash, and the excitement and enthusiasm quadrupled. Every hat in the house waved frantically: every banner and flag tossed wildly. Round after round of applause went up as he came down the centre aisle on the arm of Col. Theo G. Barker. . . . The applause giving way to cries of 'Hampton! Hampton!'"[6] The next night the reaction was the same: "Everybody knew it was Hampton before they saw him, for that crowd would not have shouted half that loud for anybody else on North American soil. All hats came off at the instant, and as he entered the quadrangle and approached the stage a scene such as nothing can describe ensued. The people beheld their idol. . . . They all cheered. Some of them shed tears. Some of them choked with emotion and could do nothing more than raise their hats in silent homage. It was a scene that none who witnessed will ever forget."[7] It is not hard to picture Wade Hampton in his Confederate gray riding atop a sturdy mount down Charleston's Meeting Street in the 1895 parade and conclude that Arno Mayer was correct when he wrote, "If anything, the use of old-world attire, transport, and splendor intensified the spell of meticulously staged pageants in tradition-soaked societies." These ceremonies "reinforced hegemonic ideas, values, and feelings that braced the prebourgeois elites."[8]

Confederate reunions offered South Carolina's conservatives great opportunities to dramatize conservative values wrapped in Confederate gray and to bolster economic improvement. As more northerners began to winter in the South, South Carolina, Charleston especially, moved to take advantage of the "history" market. As Walter Edgar has noted, "Celebrating the Old South was good business for the New South."[9] The Young Men's Business League often led the drive in Charleston to bring Confederate conventions to the city. In 1896 the league noted with pride their efforts in sponsoring the 1895 Confederate reunion, initiating an effort to "build and equip a cotton mill in our city," and having supplied "material aid, in managers and polling places" for a local election to exempt manufacturing from local taxes for five years.[10] The league continued to promote historic Charleston for its tourist and convention potential. While this was not quite the power of history Frederick Porcher and other mid-nineteenth-century southern conservatives had in mind, good business would surely help keep good order. With the building of the Charleston Naval Yard (with federal money), a growing textile industry, and recovering cotton prices, Charleston and the lowcountry began to experience actual economic prosperity in the early 1900s.

Conservatives such as Theodore Jervey Jr. nonetheless found plenty of problems remaining in these new economic times. Despite a brief fling in the early 1890s with progressive-style optimism, Jervey by the beginning of the new century pushed his search for order well beyond the cautious hopefulness of the progressives. Jervey fancied himself a gentleman writer, producing works of fiction and more scholarly works on race. As Jervey's elitism deepened through the early 1900s, his perspective widened through study and acquaintances to sympathize with European imperialism. At home he concluded that both African Americans and poor whites were largely beyond help. Fortunately, he believed, conservatism might be bolstered in South Carolina by the unstoppable forces of capitalism and timely recognition by powerful Europeans of the need for elite rule.

Theodore Jervey Jr. was born in 1859. He later was described by Ulrich B. Phillips as "a Charlestonian of the strictest loyalty."[11] Jervey's earliest memories were of the final days of the war and coming, as he explained, "to an appreciation of what was happening in this world just when the independent government of the Southern states was reeling to its fall."[12] His memories of his teenaged years included the return to "home rule" in 1876, when "Hampton rescued the State."[13] A graduate of the Virginia Military Institute, Jervey became a lawyer in 1881. Jervey's father was a prominent Charleston banker who for a while held the influential position as collector of customs for the Port of Charleston. Backed by family wealth, Jervey practiced law and became the Charleston police recorder, a minor magistrative post, in the 1890s. His career as a writer can be divided into two phases. In the late 1880s and early 1890s Jervey began his career as a reformer by championing the cause of Ben Tillman and the aspirations of "the people." When the Tillman administration, true to its word, persisted in its attack on the old regime, Jervey retreated. He spent the rest of his long life back in the conservative fold, wrestling through his writing with the "problems" of race, class, and the historical role of the elite in society.

In sharp contrast to McCrady, Jervey saw the Tillman movement of the late 1880s as a chance for needed reform in Charleston and South Carolina politics. Believing that the state's traditional leadership had grown complacent, Jervey helped lead a journalistic effort to shake up the old ruling regime, often referred to as "the ring." Jervey's desire for political reform mirrored the economic aspirations of a new generation of local leaders that Don Doyle has identified.[14] Whether it was business or politics, a new group of educated young men, many with old Charleston names, decided that "change" was in the air. In 1888 Jervey accepted the position of editorial writer for a new, rival newspaper in Charleston, *The World*.[15] His efforts on behalf of *The World* did not escape the notice of his ever-vigilant fellow Charlestonians. One letter noted that "Mr. Theo. D. Jervey, Jr. has recently appeared in the role of a ring smasher. . . . Mr. Jervey's friends are somewhat puzzled at the stand he has taken." While the author could not doubt Jervey's sincerity, he also could not help adding that the Jervey family was well established within the very "ring" Jervey was attempting to dismantle: "It's nothing to his discredit, but his family name appears rather prominently in the role of public officials, and there is some curiosity to know if he is aiming at them."[16]

If not aiming at specific family members, Jervey was certainly aiming at the older generation. While older conservatives such as McCrady saw the rise of Tillman as an annoying by-product of too much democracy, some younger Charlestonians welcomed it as a chance to reform the political system. The two generations of conservatives parted momentarily over their faith in "the people." One would have been hard-pressed during these years, for instance, to find an article on politics in the *News and Courier* such as that run under the title "The Public Is No Fool" by *The World*.[17] Frederick Porcher, Edward McCrady, the *News and Courier,* and the older generation of conservatives all believed firmly that "the public" was indeed foolish. This was precisely why society needed a small, talented, and trained ruling elite and why McCrady had reiterated the year before on behalf of traditional conservatism that "the public business is ours!"[18]

Striking a theme maintained throughout the paper's short life, Jervey and *The World* called for help from "all its progressive citizens"; they added that urban improvement, economic progress, and the open exchange of ideas comprised the ingredients for success, provided that "the people are intelligent enough to criticize themselves."[19] Naive to the meaning being taken from Tillman's rhetoric in the backcountry, "the people" meant to Jervey and *The World* individuals like themselves—educated, urban professionals impatient with the traditional regime of their fellow family members.[20] The "great revolution" they proclaimed in 1888 was, in fact, a modest wish for a "champion of political right and honest methods . . . fair dealing in politics and purity everywhere."[21] Their personal frustration with the old-style conservative rule allowed them to misread wildly Ben Tillman's explicit attacks on the traditional ruling elite. Their desire for reform in South Carolina went little beyond wishing for the time when "the young men of the state will take hold of the affairs of the commonwealth, political, commercial, and general."[22]

In September 1888 the old conservative guard still possessed the strength to dominate the state Democratic convention, and Tillman announced his "retirement" from politics. True to his word, Jervey through *The World* proclaimed that the proceedings had been fair and easily accepted the outcome. He could not resist adding that "an infusion of new blood and new brains have been needed, and it is now exceedingly gratifying to see its materialization." Pleased with their generation's inclusion in the proceedings, they declared that the political openness they desired for the state had been achieved. *The World* displayed the hopefulness of early southern progressivism through its predictions, variations of which were repeated throughout the life of the paper: "South Carolina has a great work for her young men to perform in the management of affairs of the state, politically and materially." The old ruling traditions were to be "reformed and purified," while political openness was "fostered and encouraged." With the rise of young men, "ring-rule will disappear and factions dissolve" and an informed electorate would, under their leadership, coalesce calmly into "a common majority."[23]

Jervey and *The World* took pains to prove to their older, conservative Charleston rivals that the paper was a safe voice for reform. Proudly the newspaper ran a lengthy interview with Robert Aldrich, a Barnwell lawyer and later a circuit court judge, as "a conservative opinion from one of the state's most prominent men." (The paper could have added to Aldrich's credentials that he seconded Wade Hampton's nomination for governor in the stormy campaign of 1876.) Aldrich, the paper reported, analyzed the Tillman movement as a reaction by a liberty-loving people against a ruling class whose "methods have been faulty" in recent years. "Instead of the people choosing their own servants," Aldrich continued, "they have had candidates in which they have had little or no voice in the selecting, forced upon them with the alternative, 'take these or go to the Radicals.'" Much as *The World* had been saying for the past two years, Aldrich characterized Tillmanism as "a policy by which the people will in fact, as well as in theory, choose their own servants. He offers to the people self-government, pure and simple." Aldrich added that there was little for the older conservatives to fear from a Tillman administration: "Men like him, while bold and aggressive in the fight for power, are proverbially conservative once they have gained it." *The World* also used Aldrich to defend implicitly its claim as "The People's Paper." Addressing the conservative concern that an open primary system would degrade South Carolina candidates, compelling them to undertake popular campaigns, the interviewer asked Aldrich: "You think, then, that hereafter all candidates will have to get down to personal electioneering for the offices they aspire to?" Aldrich responded grandly, "I do not think it much of a descent to get on the plane of the sovereign people." [24]

A letter from "Agricola" also supported *The World*'s efforts for Tillman as a safe movement for reform. "Some of the broadest and most liberal minds of the state are wishing and working for its success," wrote Agricola, "and I would add that they are safe and conservative men as well." Arguing that the people were not only sovereign but competent, Agricola added that if "the farmers" were indeed the backbone of the state, "their backbones must presumably be surmounted with brains enough to safely and conservatively do their own thinking."[25]

After Tillman's victorious campaign in 1890, Jervey and *The World* parted with the new administration with revealing suddenness. Nominated as executive chairman of the Charleston Democratic Party organization by the "reform" faction, Jervey encountered opposition from a nominee of the "ring" faction (or "regular" faction, according to the *News and Courier*). To settle the dispute, Tillman offered a plan, an "ultimatum." This called for a local commission on elections that included members of both factions. After years of Tillman's attacks on all things Charleston, Jervey and *The World* seemed genuinely surprised by the new governor's willingness to let the city's Democrats fight with one another awhile.[26] Jervey became chairman of the local Democratic Party, but the experience shattered his delusions about movements for change. Tillman was not the pure reformer *The World* had hoped he would be. Jervey learned that good governance, apparently, involved more than just opening to the public a free exchange of ideas and a greater voice. Voters' support of Tillman and especially of Cole Blease later proved to Jervey the ability of the people to elect bad governors. *The World* closed its door late in 1891, and in 1895 Jervey joined the city government as the police recorder, as he wrote self-critically, "putting niggers in jail, six days a week for a monthly consideration."[27]

By the early 1900s South Carolina's progressives were hard at work putting the democratic genie set loose by Tillman back in the bottle. Historians David Carlton, Walter Edgar, and Robert Milton Burts have shown the different ways that the state's conservative brand of progressivism imposed the values of an educated, wealthy elite over the lives of the poor.[28] Gerrymandering, the creation of city commission governments, and at-large voting helped insure that the mill hand and otherwise poor and white voters would not actually wield much political power. Theodore Jervey contributed to the conservative picture of the early 1900s in a different way. In his incarnation as a writer, Jervey represented what Daniel J. Singal described as the southern "post-Victorians" of the early 1900s who "reached out to 'realism' in one form or another" but who ultimately "could not bring themselves to part with the mythology that gave them their principal identity as southerners and that embodied the cultural values most dear to them." For southern post-Victorians, and certainly for Jervey, modern systems of thought such as progressivism, "to the extent that they truly absorbed them—may have provided some perspective on their society, but none of these theories proved sufficient to overcome their most deeply grounded beliefs."[29]

Not unlike South Carolina's progressives, Jervey grew more obsessed with the "race question" after African Americans had been disfranchised than he had been when they were still a viable part of the political state. By the early 1900s drafts of essays he was working on dealt specifically, almost exclusively, with "the negro question."[30] Despite what white South Carolinians had rationalized to one another, the disfranchising results of 1895 did not quell racial tensions. In 1900 rumors spread that Sumter's black community, angered by the recent killing of a black trainman by a white conductor, had gathered in the woods to plan an assassination campaign of local prominent whites, and these rumors prompted the Sumter Light Infantry to gather in defense of an attack that did not materialize. Also in 1900 white toughs in Columbia broke up a parade and drill ceremony of the black Capital City Guards and their guests, the Savannah Light Infantry, on the statehouse grounds. After a fight ensued, the black militia company was fined and disbanded by order of the governor.[32] Incidents such as these kept conservatives' search for order in full motion. The struggle between the conservative beliefs in elite rule over all and beliefs in white supremacy over black South Carolinians drove Jervey to search for solutions in the European imperialist regimes in Africa. Jervey's efforts also brought him into an unusual friendship by mail with the notorious African American author William Hannibal Thomas.[31] Not convinced that segregation had solved much of anything, especially considering segregation's Tillmanite origins, Jervey began to work through his concerns by writing a book of historical fiction.

Jervey's 1905 novel, *The Elder Brother,* is a thinly veiled account of war, Reconstruction, and "Redemption" in Charleston. Its subtitle asserts that while the work is fiction, its descriptions of life after the war were nonetheless true: *A novel in which are presented the vital questions now confronting the South growing out of Reconstruction, and in which the author defines the true relations between the races now existing in the South.*[33] Jervey's self-proclaimed realism and his assertion of the book's validity as a realistic description of South Carolina convinced the *New York Times* reviewer, who wrote that *The Elder Brother* was "astonishingly and microscopically true in its substance." Jervey, the reviewer continued, was "a photographer of facts" and "exceedingly temperate and moderate."[34] *The Elder Brother* gave Jervey the opportunity to explain how and why segregation and disfranchisement had settled the race issue temporarily if imperfectly. With his reformer days behind him, Jervey's conservative beliefs ran through the novel: African Americans could not handle freedom; government under simple white rule was limited in its capacity to secure social stability in a biracial society; and a healthier appreciation for the older generation of southern leaders would ameliorate problems generated by both of the above.

Set in "Ellenton," a fictionalized Charleston, the story focused on how an elite southern family consisting of a widower and his two sons made their way through the confusing postwar years.[35] Jervey used the father, Berwick Gordon Sr., to construct the conservative model. Gordon was "Southern to the core" and "a purer, higher type of manhood"; he had fought in the war, of course, but survived "with no animosity toward the Northern people— indeed, saw much that was admirable in them"; and he had owned slaves but was "glad" that slavery was gone.[36] Jervey depicted Gordon's affection for his former slaves as unchanged by emancipation. His two sons, Rupert and Berwick Jr., reached adulthood during Reconstruction, thus adding a coming-of-age theme to the narrative. The sons took up occupations that mirrored Jervey's career: the oldest was a journalist and local politician; the younger an attorney.

Within the melodramatic narrative, Jervey asserted his belief that the freedmen were ill-prepared for political participation. The distinctions Jervey created among his African American characters all had to do with their political activism and reflected his conservative inheritance dictating that slaves and their descendants who kept their place deserved affection and care. Those black characters who behaved otherwise Jervey cast in portraits dripping with the ugliest racism. A postwar Republican county convention was "thronged with negroes . . . well-dressed young mulattoes, who aped the whites to the very latest style and manner, and woolly savages from the adjoining islands, whose clothes were almost all that could distinguish them from their brethren in Africa." Jervey described the black members of an audience at a political debate as including some "negro mechanics, fairly intelligent men." But the rest, "in far greater numbers, were thieves and vagrants, ne'er-do-wells from the surrounding county and all the riff-raff of the city." As their spokesman recounted the war for emancipation, "The wilder negroes from the islands howled in unison, while the saliva fairly glistened on their tusks as they glared at the whites whom they remembered as master."[37]

Descriptions of specific black characters included that of a political leader named B. F. Porter, described as "a quarrelsome, vindictive, insolent, treacherous negro." Revealingly, Jervey stressed explicitly that political aspiration made Porter "completely spoiled for all work." "Colonel" Sam Jenkinson, another black politician, "was a bricklayer before the war, but since then had set up for a lawyer, and having some homely wit he made a buffoon of himself before court and jury whenever he could obtain the opportunity." Involved in a street struggle, Jenkinson appeared "with his ape-like face distorted with passion . . . all the more ape-like under the nodding plumes of his hat." Employing the conservative interpretation of emancipation already nationally recognized among whites, Jervey noted that with freedom, "a vast number utterly incapable of understanding the difference between liberty and license had been thrown upon the world, a law unto themselves. . . . Work, they had long since discarded."[38]

The depiction of black characters of whom Jervey approved contrasted sharply to these lurid descriptions. Noticeably the characters he portrayed positively had lived long under slavery, remained tied to their former masters through the bonds of affection, and had little taste for politics. Jervey depicted Bonaparte, a former slave who had followed his master through the war. Bonaparte's faithful service to his master only "confirmed the contempt which he seemed to feel for the bulk of his own race." Along the same lines, Washington, a former slave of the Gordon family, maintained "a love [for the Gordon children] he could not feel for his own children." Jervey narrated Washington's thoughts as he contemplated the political struggles of the freedmen following the war: "What was all the trouble? Why did the negroes wish to rule? He was content to be free, his own master, and surely if ever there was a fool, Sam Jenkinson was one." Yet, Washington conceded, "many of the negroes would vote for Sam Jenkinson or Porter to make laws, rather than for a white man." Jervey then completed his construction of Washington as an acceptable freedman from the conservative white perspective. Washington, Jervey wrote, "did not wish to make any laws, because he knew he could not." "Was it possible," Washington asked himself, "as some of the negroes declared, that if the whites regained the rule, slavery would be restored? Washington did not think so." Finally, almost tearfully, the humble Washington turned to Rupert Gordon, the white aristocratic son, for advice, asking, "What can I do? My people are all for this yere man Coles, and I believe they will kill any black man who don't vote with the black people; but if you and your pa say so, I will vote for Colonel Everard, or Mr. Bohun, or any of those gentlemen, no matter what happens." Rupert counseled emphatically, "Don't vote at all, and keep out of the way, for there is very apt to be trouble on election day." Politics, the conservative advice maintained, was a dangerous business for the ill-prepared and inferior.[39]

Jervey suggested that the better among the African American "race" accepted disfranchisement. Some had even prospered: "Freedom from politics had forced their attention toward other channels, and from it there was distinct gain in their moral and material welfare." Describing black disfranchisement as "freedom from politics" sanitized, to say the least, the struggle for white supremacy in the postwar South. Pushing the point further, Jervey asserted that the positive lessons learned under slavery still applied: "In the trades many of them had been carefully educated, as slaves." Now, "since they could no longer hope to shine and dazzle the world as makers of laws and shapers of policies," some were taking better advantage of the skills developed under slavery. "The great mass," however, "was sinking. Numbers of hale, hearty young men spent their entire time gambling, loafing and fighting, and only working when, from the criminal courts, they passed to the chain-gang."[40]

Jervey's fling with Tillmanism safely in his past, his portrayal of the old ruling elite revealed his sympathies with a traditional conservatism that crossed race and class lines. While much of *The Elder Brother* deals with postwar race relations, Jervey could not resist incorporating the conservative concerns about the state's all-white political solution. Jervey created a sympathetic character in Col. Hugh Everard, who was unquestionably modeled on Edward McCrady Jr. Colonel Everard secured passage of a law identical to McCrady's real-life Eight-Box Law. Everard also "declared from the outset that the negroes ought to stand before the courts and in the enjoyment of their political rights upon exactly the same footing as the whites; but had as positively declared that no illiterate man, be he white or black, should have the right to vote." Other conservative characters in the scene summarized Everard's (McCrady's) position as being right on principle but wrong on timing: "The matter has practically been decided for us. We cannot afford to stand in an attitude of hostility to the rest of the white population in the State. The color line has been drawn." Through this dialogue Jervey demonstrated the conservatives' awareness that holding a belief in white superiority and mounting a campaign in the name of a "whites only" democracy were not identical matters. The entire episode reveals yet another of those moments of dreaded convergence when the conservatives' fundamental racism and elitism could not be kept apart. Much as the real-life McCrady wavered, Everard later worried as his law became manipulated to favor white voters. The law, he believed, "preserves our civilization; but inasmuch as it accustoms us to the idea of fraud at the ballot-box, the idea of fraud in public office is spreading." Southern civilization was saved from a "devastating flood" of black misrule. Yet, he worried, "it may rot away slowly if we do not check this corrupting influence in time." In *The Elder Brother,* as in real life, the campaign for white supremacy prevailed, with full-scale segregation soon to follow. But traditional conservatives such as the fictional Everard, the real McCrady, and Jervey often wondered at the price.[41]

In the early 1900s Jervey and later William Watts Ball still put forward the traditional conservative view of poor whites and most African Americans. While hoping to find mechanisms that would provide some uplift, they could never completely abandon the conservative precept that some people, perhaps most people, in this life were born to be poor and ignorant. As a result, the decades-long conservative criticism of American democracy continued.

After some modest success with *The Elder Brother,* Jervey took another turn at fiction writing, and this time he became much more openly critical of South Carolina's all-white political solution of 1895. Whereas *The Elder Brother* focused on the last days of Reconstruction, "Love Blinds?," an unpublished manuscript, revisits the lowcountry in the 1890s. Early in the story Nicholas Horbiston, a young man from an elite coastal family, described his home and surroundings to his northern-born college roommate, Thomas Ashe. The community consisted of six or seven large families, "the remaining holders of large tracts of land, planted by them with the aid of slave labor before the war." Freedom, Nicholas explained, had not driven away the former slaves, who along with their descendants "remain . . . in the main docile, quiet and well behaved . . . needing guidance and instruction."[42]

In a characterization working as a stinging rebuke of the premise behind the post-1895 all-white democracy, Jervey has Nicholas describe the poor whites in the area as "owners of a few acres of pineland and swamp, living by hunting and stock-raising, a shiftless set, rather loose in their morals." Jervey narrates that unfortunately poor whites, "through their possession of the ballot," represented "a force, the negroes do not possess." Jervey's young aristocrat Nicholas laments, "If you take the opinion of most of the planters, you will find them very nearly hopeless of ever elevating either negroes or crackers." Later, traveling inland from the coast, Nicholas observed that the land became "poorer at every mile." The homes of those they met were small and ramshackle, "with little to distinguish the dwellings of whites from blacks." Along the way he saw a young white woman in her teens, "dirty and ill kempt," wearing a "wretched formless shift" and no hat. On her head lay "a thick and tangled mass of yellow hair." Jervey concluded this scene, however, by combining his description of this poor creature with a hint at sexual tension. As the carriage in which Nicholas rode went past, he recalled how she stared at the travelers while "with one bare foot she lazily scratched the dirty brown well developed calf of the other leg, just as an animal might have done."[43]

Jervey wrote into Nicholas's character the belief that enfranchised poor whites remained confounded by the legacy of white superiority generated by the institution of slavery. "These people," he continued, "present the strongest indictment ever framed against slavery. They are still despised by the negroes, whom they hate intensely." Poverty stretched the bonds of race thin. As a member of the local elite, Nicholas observed that poor whites "distrust us and all our ideas." He concluded his social commentary with the summary that "as a class, just in proportion to the number of slaves about them, they seem to have sunk first to a pastoral and then a savage life . . . it seems to me that in this coast region, being an absolute cipher in our civilization, all pride, ambition and religious perception was destroyed in these people."[44]

The prominent South Carolina historian David Duncan Wallace, a contemporary, shared Jervey's portrayal of poor whites but blamed Ben Tillman for having "worked the fetish of Anglo-Saxonism too hard." The result was that "our ignorant people have been told so often that they are the grandest people on the face of God's earth that too many of [them] concluded that raw Anglo-Saxonism is all sufficient, regardless of education and character." Poor whites, as a result of the campaigns for white supremacy, had taken on "a supreme self[-]satisfaction" and an "egotistical contentment with themselves as they are." This inflated self-opinion, he continued, led in turn to their "passionate rebellion against any attempt to improve that which by this logic can need no improvement." Indeed this presented a conundrum for white southern conservatives such as Jervey and progressives such as Wallace. If the white race were superior, why did *some* whites need *so much* reform?[45]

When a subplot to "Love Blinds?" featured a local religious leader whose mission was to reform the moral character of poor whites in the area, Jervey again provided a view common among the local elite. Nicholas Horbiston's neighbor, Mr. Lane, thought little of the reform efforts, asserting that "to be a genuine Christian, one has to get perilously near socialism. That is all very well for a priest, but the very devil for a planter." The missionary to the poor whites, Arthur Pearson, knew what he was up against. Lamenting how "the feeling of caste is inculcated by one's surroundings and hereditary influences," he was not surprised that the local aristocrats doubted his association "with the class our progenitors regarded with such contempt." Jervey, however, gave the last word in this scene to young northerner Thomas Ashe. Ashe agreed with his elite hosts: "From the ranks of the classes come always the wisest and greatest champions of the rights of the masses; just as from the masses, the classes recruit their most doughty men at arms. I don't believe Democracy ever received more loyal service than was rendered by the aristocratic representatives of the South in the first three or four decades of the Constitutional life of this Republic." In Jervey's portrayal, leadership by the elite, imperfect though it was, remained vital to the advancement and stability of society.[46]

Near the end of "Love Blinds?," Jervey made a striking connection between race relations in South Carolina and those in South Africa at the turn of the century. Jervey sent Nicholas Horbiston's un-Reconstructed uncle, William Deane, from South Carolina to fight alongside the Dutch descendants in the Boer War against the British. Thomas Ashe, now Horbiston's brother-in-law, traveled to South Africa to find Uncle William. Along the way Ashe pondered how men such as William Deane, an "unreconciled South Carolinian," had "found in the Boer War a vent for their feelings concerning the Race Question and had fought it out like men." Ashe "almost wished he had been with them. Our War with Spain was but a pelting war." Stopping at Cape Town and moving on to Durban, Ashe continued to survey the conditions of South

Africa with an eye toward South Carolina. "One thing he found out," Jervey wrote for Thomas Ashe, "and that was if ever there had been a place to which the unreconciled Southerners should have gone in 1865, it was Natal. . . . Here was Negro and Coolie labor and veiled economic slavery." Had disgruntled Confederates "sore from failure of Britain to recognize the Southern States in the War of Secession" just come to Natal, the Ashe character continued, "in twenty years might they not have so influenced Natal politics and the politics of the Transvaal as to have brought about a South African Union without war? The real question in Natal was, as it was in the Transvaal and the Orange River Free State, as it would eventually be in Cape Colony, the Race Question." If, Ashe concluded, "a great humanitarian statesman, Gladstone, was ready to welcome into the family of Nations an independent, slavocratic, cotton producing country in North America, why not in South Africa? That was just the place for such."[47]

With an insightful grasp of the contradictions at the very inception of the Jim Crow South—when, just as conservatives feared, good governance did not seem automatically to replace the ousted black voters—Jervey through *The Elder Brother* and "Love Blinds?" labored with the problem of a state divided along racial lines but governed by a citizenry that included poor and uneducated whites still sensitized to race matters. Jervey eventually advocated a more radical solution, invoking the power of capitalist market forces to the "race problem" by encouraging African Americans to leave South Carolina. Jervey's intellectual efforts toward this end culminated in the 1925 publication of *The Slave Trade: Slavery and Color*.[48]

Unlike works of fiction that explored through stereotypes and melodrama the lowcountry since the Civil War, *The Slave Trade* represented a more scholarly effort to fit a modern, mobile American society within a living and, to Jervey, worthwhile tradition of elite rule over matters of race.[49] The standard interpretation of slavery in the early 1900s praised the Old South for its economic and political achievements as well as its stabilizing effects on both races. Jervey in *The Slave Trade* concurred that slavery succeeded as a means of racial control, but he also expressed that this was no cause for great praise. He argued, instead, that the assertion that slaves were also property stirred fundamental human greed and in turn fostered the unhealthy racial population distribution still plaguing the South. Jervey therefore questioned praise for the achievements of the plantation economy. He interpreted the development of the Old South as an unhealthy by-product of antebellum market forces. He also anticipated that twentieth-century market forces may yet prove to benefit the local elite's desire for control over blacks and poor whites.

Early in *The Slave Trade,* Jervey asserted that at the constitutional conventions of the 1780s the Negro question "first really arose" with unfortunate consequences for the South. In creating the new nation with slavery intact, the Founding Fathers sidestepped an issue that Jervey believed still plagued the South, "the mere presence in the Republic of a large and growing number of people of an inferior race." Following independence, the desire for property and its protection continued to blind white southerners to the problems of growing black numbers. By 1840 "the property interests in Negroes had become so immense, that it not only paralyzed other industries . . . but it affected public opinion to a degree which now seems hardly credible." Jervey explained straightforwardly that "the continual increase of the Negro population and the immense sums invested in that species of property had worked a disintegration of former views" that slavery was a necessary evil. Market forces dominated. "Interest will color opinion," Jervey asserted, "and Negro cheap labor is still the first consideration to many people in the South, just as European pauper labor is to many in the North." Armed now with a dubiously reasoned "slavery as a good" philosophy, South Carolina grew into the "great upas tree" under which "all greatness languished." Jervey parted from most white southerners of the early 1900s by placing the blame for the South's misguided thinking on John C. Calhoun. Calhoun, Jervey argued, "fastened upon the South" a passion for slavery by proclaiming the black race "the best substratum of population in the world and the one on which commonwealths may be most easily and safely reared." Jervey concluded that "once it was accepted, the march was steadily on to disaster."[50]

While slavery was destroyed, the issue of the black population lingered long after the war and the overthrow of Reconstruction. As he moved the reader toward the 1890s, Jervey found support for his views on the racial "diffusion" in the words of prominent conservatives and former Confederate generals Wade Hampton and Matthew C. Butler. Invoking Confederate heroes was more than the perfunctory genuflection at the altar of the Lost Cause. Of Hampton and Butler, Jervey reminded his readers that "both were members of families which had been identified with the history of . . . South Carolina from the Revolutionary War. Both belonged to the slave-holding planter class. Both had served with distinction in the Confederate War, rising respectively to the grades of lieutenant general and major general." Both also argued in the

1890s that African Americans should move out of South Carolina. Jervey not only protected himself through the words of Confederate generals, but he established that a challenge to him was a challenge against the best of the Old South.[51]

Jervey's views on the removal of the state's black population mixed traditional white southern fears of miscegenation with an awareness of a European imperialism that increasingly used racial justifications for colonial aggression. For Jervey, fewer numbers of the "inferior race" would mean simply fewer opportunities for interracial sex. He had read in H. M. Stanley's *In Darkest Africa* proof of the evils of miscegenation. From Stanley's reports of biracial villages in East Africa, Jervey noted, "The superior race has not avoided miscegenation, but, upon the contrary, it has steadily progressed, until distinctions in color are almost gone . . . and this miscegenation seems to have checked progress in civilization." In this context, civilization meant white to Jervey. Any "mixing" that diluted whiteness was by definition a step away from being civilized. The biracial villages described in *In Darkest Africa* suffered, by Jervey's reasoning, from "a reduction to what is practically two classes of Negroes, as far as to the outside world is concerned."[52]

The situation Jervey found in Stanley's writing contrasted sharply with the life of South Africa's Boers. Jervey openly admired the Boers' racial views and claimed an intellectual kinship. He noted with pleasure that "the Englishman . . . is just commencing to see some of the virtue of the Boer who, until recently, has shared with the South Carolinian the distinction of being the most vilified of all people." Jervey observed that the Boer, "like the South Carolinian, believes that, between the races, 'familiarity breeds contempt.'" He expressed clear satisfaction that beginning in the late 1800s, "a great change of sentiment was taking place in the world." The Western powers of Great Britain, Germany, and the United States were abandoning their "extravagantly liberal and humanitarian ideas, with regard to the race question, which had marked the twenty-five years preceding 1890." These misguided notions now gave way to "race-imperialism." He pointed out that it was, after all, "England . . . that altered the designation of 'The Brother in Black' to 'The White Man's Burden.'"[53]

Jervey also noted the similarities between the German imperialist writer Paul Rohrbach's ideas and John C. Calhoun's "sub-stratum" theory.[54] In *German World Policies,* Rohrbach wrote of the German presence in East Africa, "If the fact of a division of labor between the white and black people in our African colonies is thus established, it is obvious that the black must be the serving people, and the white constitute the upper class."[55] Jervey's study of European imperialism included French colonialism in Senegal. Privately in 1926 he described Senegalese leader Blaise Diagne as "this most remarkable French colored man."[56] Jervey's praise makes sense. By the mid-1920s Diagne, the first African to be elected to the French Parliament, was lecturing young Senegalese on their lack of respect for Europeans and "respectable folk."[57]

Having proclaimed his admiration for the Boers and the German imperialists, Jervey turned his focus back to South Carolina. His conservative perspective allowed him to be critical of both the Tillman government and contemporary black leaders. "In every way in 1890," he explained, "the Negro seemed to have failed." At home, however, powerful forces conspired to thwart racial diffusion in the 1890s, and millions of black people remained in the South. Jervey lamented the Tillman administration's South Carolina act of 1891 that restricted the freedom of black mobility and punished northern labor agents recruiting cheap black labor. As Frederick Porcher had learned by 1865, this was a futile attempt to hold "natural" market forces at bay. Jervey added that not surprisingly, it was legislation "which her wisest sons had unavailingly opposed." Yet, he mourned, it fit the short-term needs of "the white agriculturalists of the Lower South . . . to hobble, within their reach, cheap Negro labor."[58]

Jervey believed that the "race" leadership of Booker T. Washington threatened subtly the elite's ability to control white supremacy locally. Unlike many educated white southerners of the early 1900s, Jervey disagreed with the views of the popular African American leader. Washington advised black people to stay in the South, precisely the opposite of Jervey's wishes. Jervey bemoaned on behalf of "the Negro" the "active, continuous, well financed propaganda, led by the most influential member of the race, that he should cling to the South." In addition to that more obvious disagreement over where black people should live, Jervey also understood the implications of Washington's views and saw much more in him than a popular conciliator. Washington, Jervey observed, did not completely renounce the wish of African Americans for social equality and civil rights. As Jervey noted, "He condemned the agitation, not the aspiration for it."[59]

Before concluding *The Slave Trade,* Jervey indicated that there was hope after all. As Frederick Porcher's postwar conclusions first indicated, southern conservatives now accepted, to some degree, the bourgeois liberal view of the economy as a force larger than local determination of social arrangements. Jervey attributed the black migration beginning in World War I to the natural pull of an industrialized economy. These natural workings of the economy now produced a more sanguine racial situation in the South. According to Jervey, the year 1925 marked the first time in a century that South Carolina's white population outnumbered its black population. With "the need for brawn and sinew being felt in the North and West," Jervey wrote, "in obedience to its demand, the Negro, for a consideration, was moving out of 'his natural home.'" Jervey relished the irony of black workers migrating to the North to fill the ranks of cheap labor needed by northern industry. After all, he noted, northern concern for the former slave had over the years "gradually become restricted to assisting in fitting him for a residence in 'his natural home, the South.'" Now, Jervey pointed out, northern industry was doing what northern philanthropy dared not—it was bringing black people to the North.[60]

Idus A. Newby's analysis suggests that Jervey's observations had some merit. Black migration drew over seventy thousand out of South Carolina in each of the first two decades of the twentieth century. Then over two hundred thousand black Carolinians left between 1920 and 1930. Black migration, says Newby, contributed to a "relaxing of white racial fears" and until the Great Depression "helped alleviate the social and economic problems of black Carolina."[61]

By the end of *The Slave Trade,* Jervey had asserted into the mid-1920s some of the basic principles of traditional southern conservatism. His elitism flourished later in life when, as Porcher and McCrady might have warned him, the results of "the people" having political power proved confounding and disappointing. Jervey championed Tillman and open politics. The victorious Tillman rebuffed him personally, and the Tillman administration passed laws Jervey thought disastrous and against the people's self-interest. Years later Tillman chided Jervey accurately for distancing himself from the movement: "You yourself seem to be unable to throw off wholly the influence of the atmosphere in which you have been reared." [62] By the 1920s Jervey clearly longed for the days of leadership under Old South heroes such as Generals Wade Hampton and Matthew Butler. As a reformer interested in race, his abstract wishes for "diffusion" carried with them few specific plans. He attributed the black migration of the early 1900s solely to the inexorable forces of a market economy. The market encouraged migration and produced, in his eyes, the positive results he had expected all along. As a believer in white supremacy, he was only too happy to see African Americans leave the state. William Watts Ball, on the other hand, observed the changes wrought by the world war and arrived at a different conclusion from within the conservative perspective. During World War I, Ball witnessed war mobilization at home and socialist agitation abroad and perceived dangers abounding for the future of local, white rule.

How Can One . . . Not Be Tory or Junker?

William Watts Ball and the War Years, 1914—1945

In April 1916 William Watts Ball recorded in his diary some playful banter exchanged that day with his wife, Fay, regarding a recently passed Florida law that prohibited white teachers from teaching in black schools. When William suggested that her support of the measure indicated race prejudice, Fay Ball shot back, "Well I don't believe in slavery, but I do believe in holding the negroes down." William Watts Ball, enjoying the exchange, added in his diary that his wife's response was "a spontaneous and perfectly natural avowal of the almost unanimous Southern opinion, white, about the negroes." While Fay Ball's retort does seem to have required little reflection, William Watts Ball's assertion that her views were "perfectly natural" and "almost unanimous" reveals his own attempt to absorb traditional conservative views on racial hierarchy into the segregated South of 1916.[1]

Born in 1868, Ball descended from a wealthy upcountry family, part of the state's traditional conservative elite, and he claimed to have remained "steeped in their opinions and prejudices . . . rejecting nothing."[2] But here he invoked the Old South to explain what was a modern racial arrangement— segregation. Ball's connection to the Old South *is* clear, however, when one adds his pressing fear of poor whites. Far more than Jervey did, Ball in the early 1900s incorporated his traditional elitism within the southern progressive outlook that sought to improve the stability and prosperity of a segregated, industrializing South Carolina. The United States' entry into World War I shattered the confidence that Ball shared with other southern progressives of the early 1900s. American participation in the war, it appeared, unleashed forces toward centralization, mass democracy, racial equality, even socialism. To Ball, these forces undermined segregation while encouraging poor white political participation and further threatened to take local matters out of local hands.

Whereas Theodore Jervey thought he detected a ray of hope for elite rule in the 1920s, longtime newspaper editor William Watts Ball saw nothing but trouble. Despite the impressive rise of the textile industry, 80 percent of the state's population remained rural, living out where over 40 percent of the state's improved land grew cotton. In short, most South Carolinians relied on growing and selling cotton. This spelled disaster in the 1920s. With World War I over, cotton and tobacco prices collapsed, and farmers lost money every year throughout the decade. As late as 1930, even as Charleston, Myrtle Beach, and Hilton Head were becoming shining resort spots for wealthy northerners, 98 percent of South Carolina's farmers worked with mule-driven implements. The changes unleashed by World War I prompted an antimodern, religious reaction that set apart even conservatives such as Ball. South Carolina's Christian fundamentalists fulminated throughout the 1920s against such modern evils as movies, dancing, swimming pools, evolution, and golfing on Sundays. It was at times more than Ball's sister, Sarah Ball Copeland, could bear. She wrote from Laurens that "there is the most sickening orgy closing in this town tonight," referring to a Christian revival meeting, and adding "the Baptists are surely the most ignorant people in the world." The local fundamentalists, she noted, were "without education and many of them without intelligence," and by the end of the revival they were "so worked up that they decided that various non-conformists in town ought to be burned at the stake."[3]

Throughout his long life William Watts Ball remained a staunch conservative, although as an Episcopalian he did not share fully the antimodern view of the fundamentalists. His writings show a conservative outlook at a young age. In 1887 he gave the senior address as he graduated from South Carolina College. His speech, "Primogeniture," championed the British custom, long out of practice in the United States, of bequeathing all landed property to the oldest male heir. Ball found the primary value of primogeniture in its ability to "fix and sustain a wealthy class, a leading example of which is the English gentry." Released from the American pursuits of "getting more or in having less" money, he said, members of the English gentry were able to "kindle their talents into lights for their inferiors," a pursuit that "our railroad, cattle and cotton kings are beneath the conception of." Ball admired what he thought he saw in the British elite: "In England genius travels by the side of wealth, descending from it from father to son, its tone growing power, while it adds to beauty the dignity of age." Writing during the birth of the Tillman movement, Ball declared, "Experience shows that every nation has a wealthy class; it has been demonstrated that the fixed class is superior." (Ball's speech was made one year before Edward McCrady's similar charge in defense of elite political rule that "the public business is ours.")[4]

Following college, Ball began his long journalism career by purchasing the hometown *Laurens Advertiser* during the fires of the Tillman/Conservative political battle of 1890. He opposed Tillmanism as a naive movement on behalf of simple majoritarian rule and mass democracy. Ball started to make specific reference to the fact that as a Democrat, he was no democrat. He moved on to work for newspapers in Columbia, Charleston, Greenville, back in Laurens, and Jacksonville, Florida. When his beloved father, Beaufort W. Ball, grew critically ill in 1902, Ball returned to Laurens again to be there for his father's last days. Ball took a position with the *News and Courier* in 1904, staying until 1909 when he became managing editor of Columbia's *The State*. These were heady days for Ball. Behind the wheel of the state's largest news vehicle and living in the state capital, he adopted the southern progressive outlook popular among his fellow class of professionals.

As David Carlton has shown, progressives in South Carolina mainly sought solutions to the fast-emerging "mill problem" of the early 1900s. In addition to being a newspaper editor, Ball owned stock in at least three textile mills. His editorials and essays during the 1910s reflected his old conservative political upbringing, his current economic and political interests, and his newly found enthusiasm for progressive-style reform. The South Carolina mills often featured deplorable working conditions, as well as child labor. Textile mill owners and their backers frequently perceived an exasperating combination of ignorance and stubbornness among white workers. The willingness of mill operatives to uproot their families in search of higher wages, for instance, indicated to the owners a lack of discipline needed in the new industrial regime. For example, when the Charleston Manufacturing Company closed its doors in 1887, the *News and Courier* cited the "insufficiency and inefficiency of [white] labor" as one of the main causes of failure. Nonetheless, the mill villages springing up around the state fostered a poor white, working-class consciousness. And, as Ball and other conservatives frequently lamented, this was an impoverished, uneducated white working class with the vote. In 1910, on the strength of that mill-hand vote, Coleman Blease took the race for governor, marking a return of demagogue rule that surpassed even the Tillman years.[5]

In the midst of Coleman Blease's first term as governor—a notorious race-baiter, misogynist, and antiaristocrat—Ball cited the growing mill population as the source of the persistent political instability in South Carolina.[6] Joseph W. Barnwell, the erstwhile Charleston conservative, wrote to Ball in the midst of the Blease administration, "Who would ever have thought in 1876 . . . that we should be obliged to endure rascals of our own race and people?"[7] Writing in 1911, Ball combined a newer concern about labor radicalism with the older conservative disdain for the demagogue.[8] Could the growing labor/capital animosity among whites tempt the demagogue into reviving the black vote? Ball's answer was yes and no. "With two classes of white people," Ball worried, "the danger of coalition by one or the other with a third class apart and aloof (that third class being the Negroes) is trebled"; he tried to reassure himself that "race sympathy is so strong among whites that serious and permanent division with appeal to the Negro . . . cannot take place."[9]

Just to make sure, Ball envisioned an active state government mobilized to prevent such a divisive situation. He hoped that an elite-run state government would act to make yeoman farmers out of those tempted to become mill hands. One of the main tasks of the state, he believed, was "to make the landless South Carolinian a landlord; and the way to do this is to educate him to be an expert farmer" and a homeowner. Home ownership was more important to the state's well-being than "another cotton mill."[10] The rise of the textile industry, he feared, invited radicalism. With an eye on the mill-hand class, Ball announced to a friend during this time that he was "studying Socialism."[11] Should "the laboring man's discontent" ignite into a workers' revolution, "the wise policy is to start a counter flame to meet it, to check it, and overcome it," Ball felt, and under his brand of conservative progressivism, government played a role in fanning the "counter flame" against radicalism and disorder.[12]

Ball believed that the election of Sumter planter and banker Richard Irvine Manning as governor in 1914 marked an important victory for the forces of order and progress in the state. Thankful that the Blease regime was over, he explained that Manning's election "drives out the mosquitos and puts our people in a position to work to some purpose."[13] His essay "Back to Calhoun," written in 1917 during the Manning administration, marked the high tide of his conservative brand of progressivism. He now called for a constitutional convention that would create a progressive-style, managerial state. The focus of the new constitution, he hoped, would be on "clearing away the obstacles to reform and revision imbedded in the existing constitution," and Ball wished to see the creation of administrative boards "requiring the service of experts or specialists" for "each important department of the state." The traditional conservatism of Ball then shone through as he explained that his plan "contemplates the removal of departments . . . from factors of partisan politics so far as is possible," because "the notion that the people are fit to choose directly all officers is palpable nonsense."[14]

When not writing about how to govern, Ball frequently examined the plight of those to be governed. In a 1914 address entitled "Are the Negroes Free?," Ball gave a brief picture of African American life in segregated South Carolina. Black South Carolinians were "practically without the right of suffrage" and were denied jury duty and service in the state militia. He added, "There is no denying the plain fact that a great proportion of the white people in South Carolina hold . . . the right to visit summary punishment on the Negroes for certain crimes." Despite the obvious inequities of Jim Crow South Carolina, Ball asserted that neither African Americans nor poor whites were truly "free" because freedom rested on the foundation of property ownership: "The man with goods always gets his rights in the end—half a century from now the Negro land owners are very likely to be free politically. That is Booker Washington's gospel and it is a true gospel." Despite the likelihood of landownership by black farmers in the long run, it was at present minimal, and both poor whites and blacks remained propertyless, mired in poverty and ignorance. If, therefore, disfranchisement and being without property "makes out a case of practical slavery for the Negro, what about the poor white man—the tenant farmer particularly?" he asked.[15]

Ball noted that white tenant farmers had the vote but that "economically they are in the chains of the Negro and it is submitted that economic slavery eventually becomes political slavery." By white tenant farmers being "in the chains of the Negro," Ball meant that the presence of black tenant farmers depressed earnings of white tenant farmers. Employing crude language, he continued that the white farmer could only get "the 'nigger wage' and, meantime, he can't live like a 'nigger.'"[16] The impoverishment of white tenant farmers in turn kept the wages of white mill workers down by forming a pool of surplus labor. Privately, Ball wrote, "Our cotton mill villages are no more than little cities of refuge of poor whites run away from the farm by Coolie competition."[17] Moreover, there was always the threat, which mill owners rekindled from time to time, of hiring black workers for the mills.[18] Therefore, Ball felt that "the problem before the South is to save the poor white man" by getting property into his hands.[19]

Ball's solution also featured education and the planned immigration of whites. By raising the education level of both poor blacks and whites, "the

Negro's living standard will improve and the white man will not be dragged down." The increased competition between educated blacks and whites did not concern Ball: "We can, I hope, depend on the white's native superiority to keep ahead of the Negro." Like the Mississippi planter and writer Alfred Holt Stone, whose work he read, Ball advocated immigration of more whites to the state, suggesting "50,000 Belgians or other white men, with their families." This hearty infusion would give a further boost to the state's white tenant population, "as a class . . . a scattered and beaten people."[20]

Ball's plans again show the conservative suspicions that segregation had solved little when human weakness abounded on each side of the color line and below that which marked off the elite. As a conservative, Ball, as did Porcher and McCrady before him, accepted that a certain segment—including a large white component—of society lacked intelligence and would not enjoy financial success (Theodore Jervey was arriving at the same conclusion at the same time.) Education would help, but few conservatives predicted that it would bring the state into a new golden age of enlightenment. Ball's views also reveal again how holding views of elite rule and white supremacy could at times conflict. His assessment of South Carolina in 1914 begs asking how white tenants, as members of a superior race, had allowed themselves to become a "scattered and beaten people." Why would white South Carolinians need fifty thousand Belgians to restore them to prosperity? How would fifty thousand Belgians alleviate the problem of low wages caused by an ample labor supply? Ball's analysis of South Carolina before World War I and his occasionally far-fetched solutions are interesting not so much in their viability—as in, could they work? They reveal, instead, how fears of poor whites and the black community continued to push conservatives into a range of positions on the role of the state and the impact of capitalism.[21]

The entry of the United States into World War I presented a new challenge to Ball's and conservatives' power in South Carolina. It also shed him of his progressivism in short order. Historian George B. Tindall described this era as segregation's "apogee." Michael O'Brien agreed with Tindall's assessment of segregation resting comfortably in the white southern mind, adding that not until later, as the New Deal began to function, and "only in the volumes of sociologists, mainly from the North, did the coming tide of challenge become explicit." In contrast to Tindall's and O'Brien's conclusions, Ball, in the heat of World War I, foresaw with a keen eye many of the approaching challenges to the system of Jim Crow. Conversely, Idus A. Newby noted that for black South Carolinians, World War I "marked off a new era." The war "bestirred black Carolinians and so disturbed traditional patterns of race relations . . . that things were never the same again." Newby pointed out that the changes were not immediate. The war instead created "intimations, aspirations, possibilities" within the black community that never entirely disappeared.[22]

In January 1918 Ball noted a dangerous inconsistency in the white southern position supporting both segregation and black soldiers fighting in Europe. He felt that white southerners, anxious to bring the war to a close, "are conceding to the negroes the right to fight for the US." This spelled trouble once the war ended, and Ball was willing, essentially, to sacrifice white American lives in Europe to protect white supremacy in the South: "The negroes who fight Germany will win their freedom—little doubt of that. We Southern 'cavaliers' should not consent that negroes be soldiers—we should cling to the notion that arms is a gentleman's profession, therefore, a white man's profession!" In 1919 Ball lamented the apparent permanency of the "war amendments" in reference to the Thirteenth, Fourteenth, and Fifteenth Amendments, which addressed the status of the former slaves following the Civil War. "If any feeble thought of their repeal lingered in the South," he grumbled, "it vanished with the participation of the Negroes in the European war."[23] Concluding this theme ominously, Ball stated, "Negro veterans returned from the war will be inconvenient material for lynchers."[24]

The war was already forcing change at home. Cotton prices shot up briefly. Historian Walter Edgar notes that, "For the first time in memory tenants and sharecroppers had real disposable income."[25] In January 1918 W. W. Johnson from Union wrote Ball updating him on the new terms arranged with Ball's tenant farmers. (Ball and his wife together eventually owned around two thousand acres throughout South Carolina.)[26] Fresh off a profitable year, Johnson was having trouble setting up the new terms because "[these] husky negroes made so much money there is no getting them to do a lick of work."[27]

In August 1918 Ball noted that rising wages relieved some African American women from having to work in domestic jobs. In conversation with a friend he reiterated that "this war was setting the negroes free and . . . we Southerners would now cease to 'own' negroes." Having already established that military service would "free" African American soldiers, he added, "Negroes have been slowly getting freer with the raising of the wage scale."

Attempting to make light of the situation, Ball asked, "'Ain't it awful?' Isn't it frightful that the 'niggers' are soon to be really free?" Returning to seriousness, Ball continued, "Of course they won't be entirely free—the white race IS superior." Still he worried that while the Civil War did not "tremendously impair" the "old relation of master and slave . . . [it] is to be impaired, remodelled, largely wiped out now."[28]

The question for Ball, then, was what would take its place? For one who feared, as Ball did, the politics of non-property-owners, the staggering power of capital accumulation, the rise of centralized power to fight wars and to mitigate the harshness of capitalism, and the pervasive ideals of democracy at the heart of both American politics and economics, there were few good options in the 1920s and 1930s. World War I generated tremendous uncertainty, and seemingly far-flung international events appeared in Ball's writing as filled with relevance for South Carolina and its ability to maintain its sense of order over a segregated, relatively undemocratic society. Even with the war over, Ball worried: "The world seems still to be out of joint—when will it settle down?"[29] The Russian Revolution and the spread of a revolutionary workers' movement into central and western Europe both frightened and intrigued Ball. On the one hand, he abhorred the communist rejection of private property. Communism brought with it the worst sort of egalitarian ideals. On the other hand, southern conservatives such as Ball wondered if the Soviets could actually remain outside of the capitalist world. There was little in the post–Civil War decades to suggest to Porcher or McCrady that capitalism could be anything but withstood or shaped in certain directions. Jervey never questioned the power of capitalism and speculated that "natural" market forces were going to help elite rule in South Carolina. Ball, on the other hand, was far less sanguine about capitalism's effects locally but was equally distressed, if fascinated, by capitalism's setbacks worldwide.

Ball had always been wary of large-scale industrial capitalism, and now he worried about post–World War I labor unrest. An open opponent of what he used to enjoy calling "small 'd' democracy," he observed anxiously a world recently made safe for it. Democracy, conservatives had long believed, invited radicalism, and in 1918 this seemed borne out clearly. Ball hoped that Germany would be spared a "bloody revolution." His thoughts on Germany blended seamlessly into his worries over segregated, industrializing South Carolina. "If, by the way," he continued, "German 'democracy' of the Marxian sort, or August Bebel's sort, or [K]arl Liebknicht's [*sic*] sort shall be ascendant and our country shall be infected with it, what will our Democrats, our landowners, our planters, cotton mill owners, bankers, 'junkers,' bourgeoisie say?" Ball even began describing himself in European conservative terms: "Are there not 'junkers' in the South who still believe they own the 'niggers'? I am that kind of 'junker' to a degree—certainly I *do not* wish the negroes in South Carolina as free as I am—and I suspect few South Carolinians would willingly concede them so much freedom as I would."[30]

His thoughts two days later on Germany again turned directly into reflections on race issues at home, and once again Ball placed himself in sympathy with an international conservative community. "Revolution," he bemoaned, "has Germany in its grips, the 'Social Democrats' are in the saddle, and the danger *not* only to Germany but to all Europe is the spread of socialistic revolution." Ball believed that to guard against this threat the United States should remove its soldiers from Europe as soon as possible. "Why expose their 'impressionable young minds' to the infection of socialism?" he asked, adding, "and my question reveals that I have an ingredient of Toryism. How can one dwell in South Carolina and not be Tory or Junker? 'Democracy?' 'Pure Democracy?' Have we not the 'Afro-American' with us?"[31]

The Charleston race riot of 1919 did nothing to alleviate these fears, of course. Ball's brother-in-law, Thomas R. Waring, editor of the *Charleston Evening Post* at the time, wrote Ball a frantic letter. "The race situation is bad," Waring confessed. "We don't know what is going on among the negroes and explosions may occur at any time under our feet." Then Waring sketched out a scheme that in some ways anticipated Mississippi's State Sovercignty Commission by some thirty-five years: "A deep and comprehensive investigation, by reliable, capable and secret agents should be made of the things going on with the blacks." He pleaded to officials to make "an inquiry through the detective agencies of the government, as well as a drastic suppression of the organs of irritation."[32]

Ball also considered a point raised by then-representative James F. Byrnes on the passage of the Nineteenth Amendment guaranteeing woman suffrage. Reporting on the possibility of a new "force" bill passed for federal oversight of voting irregularities, Byrnes noted that federal officers sent to oversee black women's registration "would at the same time be supervising the registration of male voters, and their presence would insure a much greater number of registered male negro voters." Byrnes recalled South Carolina statistics from early in the century showing that there were as many as fifteen thousand more African American children than white children attending public schools. These children should now be approaching voting age. Byrnes then allowed for a higher mortality rate among African Americans but concluded, "It is certain that if there was a fair registration they would have a slight majority of voters in our State. We cannot idly brush these facts aside."[33]

Byrnes and Ball had reason to worry over the possibility of renewed black political activity. In 1915 members of the Capital City Civic League, a group of African American business leaders and "qualified electors," published an "Address to the People" which Ball, living in Columbia at the time, surely would have seen. In the address the Civic League urged fellow black Columbians to "prepare themselves" to vote. The Civic League also contacted the National Association for the Advancement of Colored People (NAACP) about organizing a local chapter, claiming to have eight hundred registered voters in Columbia. An NAACP chapter did open in 1917, and voter registration drives followed. After 1920 the Capital City Civic League and the NAACP added black women as prospective voters to be registered.[34]

Ball's fears persisted through the presidential campaign of 1920. South Carolina's economy had already begun to falter as cotton prices plunged from 40¢ per pound to 13.5¢ in less than one year.[35] The boll weevil now plagued the state's cotton growers as well. Tobacco prices went down.[36] Ball's main concern, however, was that "Big Business" would through its relentless greed provoke the working class toward radicalization. Late in the campaign he noted, "All signs are that 'Big Business' will have its own way in this approaching election." The Democrats were fumbling away the election by focusing on the League of Nations as their main issue and thus "have relieved the party of amassed wealth of the necessity of defending itself."[37] Ball's frustration reached its peak just weeks before the election: "Never before in my life have I felt so resentfully against the Wealthy class in this country as in the last 30 days. I am a 'Conservative,' a stock and bondholder in a small way, but the impudence, the arrogance, the abominable duplicity of the Republican campaign, has made me feel that—well, let Wealth save itself from strikers, hoodlums, and from juries and legislatures that 'soak' capital whenever they can."[38] Having thrown his tantrum, Ball resumed his fight against "capital-soaking" political forces.

Just behind Ball's anger at the "Big Business" class was his greater fear of labor unrest in a democratic society and its implications for issues of race. Any amount of organizing among workers threatened radicalism. As a Spartanburg mill president wrote Ball in 1916, unions made workers "disloyal to their employers, shirkers of their work, breeders of discontent, invaders of the rights of others and usurpers of property rights."[39] Analyzing current movements of American radicalism, Ball drew a revealing historical comparison: "When [William Lloyd] Garrison denounced the constitution, he was no better than a 'Red' of this generation—and Eugene Debs or 'Big Bill' Haywood, who have been convicted of treasonable utterances against the US have as good a defense as can be set up for Garrison."[40]

Ball also feared socialists' efforts within the constitutional system. Years before, Ball sketched out an essay analyzing socialism in which he observed that socialism is "avowedly political. . . . It advertises faith in the ballot." Ball worried that socialists would continue "the political struggle until the class consciousness of all laboring men is aroused and they are enlisted under the red banner. Then they will be in an overwhelming majority and will take over the government. They will amend the constitution as they choose and convert the principle means of production and exchange into the property of the social state." All of this, he feared, would be supported, of course, by the ideals of majoritarian rule and "the Socialists, the majority party, will defend the majority's rights."[41]

Ball had seen this before. Whether it was Tillman's promise to poor farmers in 1890 that, if elected, "a Legislature in sympathy will naturally follow" or the socialists' "faith in the ballot," the unwieldiness of a democratic system loomed. "The Bolshevik and extreme socialist definitions of democracy," he explained in a 1919 letter, "imply that all men and women should have the ballot." To demonstrate the "absurdity of this theory," Ball related a recent anecdote of Berlin schoolchildren demanding the vote: "This was perfectly logical; if an ignorant person should be allowed to vote solely because he is twenty-one years old, why should a clever boy of twelve . . . be denied the privilege?" Addressing affairs locally, Ball struck the same chord: "To me, most of our political woes in South Carolina since 1868 are explained by our precipitate adoption of universal manhood suffrage." (Ball signed off the letter candidly, "But may be I am a reactionary.")[42]

Ball repeated these same fears in 1934 in a letter to former Charleston mayor John P. Grace. Exchanging concerns about "the propertyless majority to control and even to vote in Socialism," Ball hoped he would again see "a legal interlacing of the suffrage and property holders. Otherwise I fear that the day will come after a few more cycles when the propertyless will dispossess the owners of homes."[43]

Adhering to constitutional government was not enough; Ball's post–World War I conservatism featured a "strict construction" argument as well. Echoing Edward McCrady's 1899 outburst about the U.S. Constitution's modern function (McCrady at that time wrote to his niece Louisa Rebecca Barnwell, "It can be written in one word 'force'"), Ball in 1923 wondered, "How long will the constitution live?" Ball feared that "the progressive, that is, the radical, perhaps will not respect its nice and rigid restrictions when they resolve to 'do things.'" It would, he argued, be "the font of wisdom for the manual workers of this day to proceed by constitutional methods . . . but will they? Will they not kick constitutions out of their path when they shall feel strong enough to do so?" [44]

The "progressive" was now "radical." Ball had traveled a revealing distance in a short time. Back in 1917 Ball himself wanted to "do things"—he wanted to rewrite the state's constitution to "remove obstacles to reform and revision imbedded in the existing constitution" and set up panels of experts as civil servants in the name of good government. Now in the aftermath of World War I it was time to "respect its nice and rigid restrictions." Not surprisingly, by the New Deal, Ball grew convinced that the constitution had been "sadly distorted" because "courts have injected into it meanings which it did not possess, setting up for it pretended 'flexibility.'" [45]

The threat of radical change lurked behind seemingly every aspect of his daily observations. The increasing presence of automobiles, for instance, signaled to Ball that prosperity and a new consumer culture were finding their way to South Carolina. Looking through the lens of white supremacy, Ball remained unimpressed with the sight of African Americans owning and driving new cars. This, he chose to believe, represented a lack of fiscal responsibility: "I hear that the negroes are not buying bonds; when the price of cotton shall be low again, as it will be, and their cars are worn out, not many of them will be able to buy new cars." Later in the same entry Ball's elitism surfaced above his considerable racism: "Were the Southern negroes a provident people, the 'race' question would have become more embarrassment to the whites during the last four years—thousands of them would have entered the landlord class, to be rich land lords at that." Despite the changes unleashed by the war, he believed that "the whites are resolved to maintain their mastery and this they will easily do." Further, Ball added, "the rougher whites require little pretext to attack negroes." Ball, of course, held himself far above "rougher whites." With fresh evidence of white-instigated violence in the aftermath of World War I—for example, the 1919 race riot in Charleston—Ball employed a set of traditional stereotypes to spread the blame around: "Nor are the negroes without fault. They are lazy, they shirk; they must be fed. . . . When they refuse to work and there is work on the farm to be done the whites lose patience." [46]

Ball remained busy through the 1920s, serving as the dean of journalism at the University of South Carolina before moving on to become editor of the *News and Courier*. Despite the professional changes, Ball continued to keep a close eye on unfolding events, especially those that even hinted at radicalism. Commenting on the 1928 presidential campaign of Socialist Party leader Norman Thomas, Ball asked himself: "How can a decent South Carolinian be a democrat, how can he believe in political justice and 'equal privileges' to all—all, white and black? These Socialists—would they be Socialists in Liberia? Perhaps so—but not I. . . . Your Socialists would blot out state lines, but I . . . would preach 'rebellion,' secession, as my fathers did, before I would consent to the 'Democratic' doctrine of equal rights to all." [47]

When in 1929 labor unrest in Gastonia, North Carolina, right across the border from South Carolina, turned up actual communists, Ball wrote to a Greenville attorney that "the movement of these communists is designed to stir the colored population of the South." "The Southern negro," he continued, "comes nearer the definition of 'proletariat' than any other American group." If the black worker was the true proletariat, Ball saw little chance of his ever expressing true working-class consciousness. Ball sketched out a situation in Gastonia that resembled Porcher's interpretation of the post–Civil War rice worker strikes in the lowcountry. Black workers, in Ball's analysis, could never actually become communists. "The strategy," Ball contended, was to "convert to the communist doctrine a few Southern white men to take the lead in organizing the negroes under European direction." [48]

Ball then fretted over the appearance of the Unemployed Councils in the textile-producing center Greenville. In February 1931, two thousand unemployed white and black workers gathered in the city and marched to a construction site suspected of hiring North Carolina workers. A portion of the workers branched off from the main march to denounce a local banker. In April, with the Greenville police present, members of the local Ku Klux Klan forced their way into an Unemployed Council meeting and roughed up the members. The police did not intervene since it was assumed that the beating would chase away the communists. [49]

During these years Ball remained in close contact with textile executives from the Greenville area and incorporated their insights into his own concerns. His diary makes note of the "recent unpleasant incidents" in Greenville, "including the alleged whipping of a woman communist organizer." Ball understood labor's predicament. Communist labor organizers would not draw the color line, for "how can labor organize and 'fight' while drawing the color line?" On the other hand, Ball also understood the feelings of most white southern workers and wrote, "How can white people in the South forbear to draw the color line?"[50]

In the 1930s the black worker did not frighten Ball nearly as much as the increasing presence of educated African Americans did. "I am steeped in 'race prejudice,'" and "I do not enjoy, I detest, association even of a few minutes, with educated negroes," he candidly admitted.[51] In this context, Ball must have deplored the message delivered by J. Andrew Simmons at a 1932 Race Relations Sunday event in Charleston. Simmons, the principal of one of the local all-black schools, spoke before a mixed audience, whom he chided for their "readiness" to accept the status quo of segregation. Recalling his own childhood, Simmons stated that segregation had been loosely enforced at first. Upon his return from getting his degree at Fisk University, however, segregation had hardened and, what was worse, was accepted "without complaint." Predictably, Simmons received a visit from three white school board members shortly thereafter. He resigned at the end of the school year and moved to become a principal in Columbia.[52] In Columbia the same year, 1932, African Americans challenged the city's Board of Commissioners of Elections for its policy of white primaries. The board ruled that African Americans could vote if they could prove that they had voted the Democratic ticket since 1876 and the election of Wade Hampton.[53]

Ball meanwhile granted that he was "by no means so stupid as to hold myself superior to all negroes, to fancy that one who has negro blood cannot be brilliant and good." But the presence of talented, intelligent black South Carolinians was enough for Ball to "wish to live in a world apart from the best of the negroes. I do not object to their success, I would not throw an obstacle in its way if only it be achieved in some other world—or country—or separate zone—than mine. Yes, give the negroes schools, give them hospitals, give them justice in trials at law, but I deny the obligation to give them an equal chance in my industry."[54]

Ball clearly preferred all race relations to be like those he had with his domestic employees. His recorded feelings about Wilson Miles, who worked for the family during Ball's years as editor of Columbia's *The State,* provide an example of Ball's expectations. When Ball moved to Charleston to become editor of the *News and Courier* in 1927, Wilson Miles stayed in Columbia, not wishing to leave his own family. Miles became employed by William E. Gonzales, whose family owned Columbia's *The State*. Gonzales and Ball were longtime friends, and in 1930 Gonzales paid Ball a visit in Charleston, briefly reuniting Wilson Miles and Ball. Recording the evening in his diary, Ball relived the "keen pleasure, mingled with regret, or sadness" with which he "welcomed Wilson." Ball described Wilson as "my man . . . my servant seventeen and a half years, simple-minded, good natured, 'handy' negro, not always faithful, not always grateful." Once fitted into acceptable stereotypes, Wilson Miles became an African American worth missing and caring about. Ball asked himself, "What are a Southern negro's 'rights' but to serve his master, to do the bidding of the white man. And what is my duty save to be kind to 'my negroes,' to protect them from the cruelties of ruffian whites so far as I can, to be generous to them in a narrow way, to look after them, to avoid hurting their feelings, asserting my mastery as a Southern white man." [55]

This was not a new view for Ball in his relations with African Americans. In a 1916 letter to a northern editor he wrote, "With my two or three negro servants, I have all I have any need for—and they belong to me almost as completely as my father's did to him." Ball hastened to add, "To be sure, they can leave my service at will . . . but there is compensation for that. I am not legally responsible for them now when they are sick." Still he admitted that this kind of relationship "means no forward movement for democracy." [56] Years later Ball reflected on those he hired during his years in Columbia. "We began housekeeping in Columbia early in November, 1910, and we had a number of negro servants in sixteen and a half years," Ball wrote, "but only three or four do I remember distinctly."[57] Even allowing for the fact that Ball, writing in 1938, was trying to recall names and faces from several years past, the conclusion cannot be escaped that the real-life African Americans he employed were lost in the narrow roles that Ball insisted on within his own thoughts.

Small wonder that during approximately the same years Ralph Ellison would begin his monumental book *Invisible Man* with his powerful prologue: "I am an invisible man. . . . I am a man of substance, of flesh and bone, fiber and liquids—and I might even be said to possess a mind. I am invisible, understand, simply because people refuse to see me." The narrator continues, "That invisibility to which I refer occurs because of a peculiar disposition of the eyes of those with whom I come in contact. A matter of the construction of their *inner* eyes with which they look through their physical eyes upon reality." [58]

In 1932 Ball published *The State That Forgot: South Carolina's Surrender to Democracy.* An assumption could be made that a book on South Carolina dealing with "surrender" would focus on defeat in 1865. But as the subtitle makes clear, Ball focuses on South Carolina's "surrender" not to the Yankees but to the principle of majority rule through the Reconstruction constitution of 1868.[59] South Carolina in the 1920s featured a burst of Confederate monument building.[60] Ball's book represents a monument of a different kind, containing several anecdotes that allowed Ball the opportunity to put words praising the days of traditional elite rule in the mouths of both former slaves and poor whites. The book amounted to Ball's most concerted and creative appeal to history as a force that could not, nor should not, be abandoned.[61] Ball intended to remind his readers of what he feared South Carolinians had "forgotten": the state's antidemocratic tradition of elite rule.[62]

The story of "Daniel" was replete with racial stereotypes and images of benevolent, traditional elite rule. As a young slave in the 1840s Daniel, Ball wrote, was considered "turbulent, resentful, rebellious." Put up for sale, Daniel was bought by "the Judge," Ball's uncle William D. Ball. Heading back to the Judge's plantation, "the young negro, clean limbed, lithe, powerful, dark, brown, bony of face and bushy of kinky hair, was moody, silent, his eyes on the ground." Before long, and predictably, Daniel "stooped, rising with half a brick in his hand drawn back to fling it." But the Judge was more than equal to the challenge—his hickory walking stick "flew first from his hand and felled Daniel." Ball wrapped up this portion of Daniel's life with a tidy, contemporary image of slavery: "Daniel picked himself up and from that moment acknowledged his master." The incident "sealed not only the bond of master and slave, but it made a covenant of two friends."[63]

Daniel's relationship with the Judge portrayed the rule of the "good master," an image important to postbellum southern conservatism. Belonging now to the Judge, and following a beating, Daniel was in the text transformed into being "quick, handy, intelligent, responsible, reliable." (Working in another stereotype, Ball noted that Daniel married "Aunt Patience" but still had "dark sweethearts on the plantation as well.") The Judge settled any incident involving Daniel because the slave had made it clear that "I ain' goin' to be whupped by the overseer." This arrangement was satisfactory to all, Ball reported, because Daniel was "useful on the plantation, and 'Old Marster' was his friend."[64]

Through the entire story of Daniel the message was clear. Daniel would only behave under the rule of the Judge, and all, including the overseer, a white person not of the elite class, agreed that this arrangement was best. When William D. Ball died in 1861, problems with Daniel resumed predictably. Daniel "had lost his master and began to give trouble." He grew insubordinate, and this phase of his life ends with Daniel, suspected of stealing, in jail "for safe-keeping, and the safety of other people." [65]

The story of Daniel underscored Ball's belief that under masters of the elite class, such as Ball's family, slaves flourished. The message could be put forth another way, for instance in the episode featuring another slave. This slave was an expert bricklayer who sold for three thousand dollars, purchased by a slave trader who was, significantly, "of the lower order." Ball got right to the disastrous conclusion: "The weather was cold and that night the new master and his slave camped by the roadside, got drunk together, and the slave died from exposure." Here slaves literally died under the rule of owners "of the lower order." [66]

Ball also relied on accounts from his mother for his understanding of slavery, although he did not begin recording her memories until 1916. Ball was comfortable with her as an authority because her memories, he noted, were similar to the stories of Joel Chandler Harris. Recording her memories into *The State That Forgot,* Ball added, "Many a southern mother had a similar experience, for 'Uncle Remus' lived on every plantation." One exchange with his mother strikes the reader now in a way quite different than Ball no doubt intended at the time. To Ball's question "Did the negroes look forward to emancipation?" his mother replied simply, "No," and then added, "or if they did, I never heard of it. They may have feared to mention the subject in the presence of white people; anyway I never heard one of them mention it." [67]

Not surprisingly, *The State That Forgot* includes anecdotes that portray Ball's belief that poor whites were also better off under the rule of the traditional elite. Ball's father, Beaufort Watts Ball, served for years on a county board that provided pensions for Confederate veterans. William Watts Ball described meeting one of these veterans several years later after his father's death. The poor, aged veteran was "a figure, with long thin locks straggling beneath a faded slouch hat, an old brown shawl about the drooped shoulders," seated by the fire in the local clerk of court's office. When the clerk pointed out to the old man that Ball was "the Colonel's son," they shook hands. Ball recalled, "He held mine a moment, dropped it listlessly, looked at me vaguely, wanderingly." Finally the old man spoke: "'You—Colonel Ball's son?' I said, 'Yes.' He spoke slowly, 'I don't know—what we poor folks—are going to do about our pensions now he's gone.' He turned his face, looked away from mine and groped for words. They came at last, chokingly: 'He was—the very best man on the hill.'" Here, as he did with his anecdotes on slavery, Ball managed to work several stereotypes bolstering the tradition of elite rule into one brief passage. To complete the picture, Ball recalled the man actually saying that poor folks did not know what to do without the guidance of their "very best man." *The State That Forgot* gave Ball the chance to bemoan the presence of modern day "Daniels" and the poor, white Confederate descendants languishing in South Carolina's mill towns and out in their desperate red hills.[68]

The Bobbs-Merrill Company published *The State That Forgot* in 1932, a time when many South Carolinians suffered economically. As Walter Edgar writes, "If Carolinians thought things could not get worse after the economic crisis of the early 1920s, they were mistaken." Cotton prices dipped to their lowest since the 1890s, the state's per capita income dropped by over 40 percent in four years. Banks and textile mills closed around the state and the city of Charleston neared bankruptcy.[69] Much in the same vein as Frederick Porcher's postwar economic philosophy, Ball, while not an admirer of American corporate power, still linked personal hardship with the unfortunate, but natural, workings of the economy. He was disgusted when the "cotton manufacturers, the corporation lawyers, men of property" supported Coleman Blease over Olin Johnston in the 1934 gubernatorial race, since Johnston hailed from the mill-hand class and sought to represent their interests in earnest.[70] While guardedly defending Johnston, Ball held out little hope that a new governor or the government generally would be able to do much good. He also wondered whether or not the crisis resulted from "the weakening, deterioration, of American character, of classes, than by economic factor," warning that character must be restored and "the notion inculcated in the people in later years that they may look to government for help in adversity must be eradicated."[71] These remarks came months before Franklin Roosevelt had taken office.

Having established what became his critique of the New Deal, Ball did not waver significantly throughout the 1930s. He broke privately with Roosevelt just two months into the first administration—far sooner than any other southern Democrat. "The 'revolution' proceeds," he growled in May 1933, adding, "The abdication of the congress, so far, is as nearly complete as it well could be." Public works programs and federal relief streamed out of Washington at a frenzied pace, and Ball stood by amazed. As Ball recognized instantly, an expanding central government operating on behalf of democratic principles threatened everything from the conservative viewpoint: elite rule, local rule, white supremacy, and the ties to South Carolina's past. Of several disturbing trends, the assumption of power by the central government was at the top of Ball's list of worries. "Since 1877," he explained, "South Carolina has controlled its internal affairs—but we are to have a multiplication of federal office-holders concerned intimately with the citizen's, the farmer's, the tax payer's affairs. . . . This, I think, makes certain a dictation from Washington . . . in state politics." How, he wondered, would a politician representing South Carolina be able to resist allying himself with the New Deal when his constituents were receiving more and more badly needed relief from Washington? They would not be able to, Ball concluded: "Now there is to be a direct dole to the states, and people who receive handouts do not inquire whether they should have them or not or even if they are getting their fair share." Character issues aside, the implications of this centralization were quite clear to Ball: "Once the federal government has distributed alms a year or two, goodbye to 'state rights' and all that sort of thing." States' rights and "all that sort of thing" meant, among other things, elite rule and segregation.[72]

Ball grew more rigid and more extreme in his views on race in the 1930s because the fundamental questions shaping these views had changed dramatically since the days of Woodrow Wilson. Ball had the luxury in the 1910s of contemplating what the best vision of a segregated South Carolina would look like. Now he sought to keep South Carolina segregated, period: "I have been 'ringing the changes' on the danger, the certainty, that the permanent success and establishment of the 'New Deal' policies . . . would deprive the South of its power to handle the 'race problem' in the manner that it has been handled since 1876. Of the truth of this, I have not the slightest doubt, centralization in Washington and the destruction of states' rights would of course cause in a little while the conferring in practice, as well as theory, of equal rights."[73] Since Ball perceived the threat to segregation emanating from the national government (and not from grassroots civil rights activism such as the NAACP), he focused intensely on its actions. Responding to a letter inquiring about the possibilities of a federal constitutional amendment against child labor, Ball explained that any amendment for any reason was out of the question. Whether the issue at hand was child labor, Prohibition, or a federal income tax, new amendments meant bigger government. "Any amendment to the federal constitution, bringing the federal government into more intimate relation with the citizen, is charged with embarrassment to the South," he explained, and "the safety of the white South, in separation and integrity, is directly dependent upon remoteness and reduction to a minimum of control centralized in Washington."[74] Ball reserved a special place in hell for Franklin Roosevelt.[75] When Roosevelt acted on behalf of civil rights, it was demagoguery and pandering for votes—no white person could seriously think the republic able to withstand mass voting by African Americans. When Eleanor Roosevelt spoke out on behalf of African Americans, she was a meddling northern woman for whom Ball had little patience: "I think they do and always have done more harm than good to the negroes by their interference."[76]

Ball's solutions on issues of race in the South occasionally turned frantic. Not unlike Theodore Jervey's fantasies of the 1920s, Ball in 1935 conceded having a wish that "of the 8,000,000 negroes in the Southern states, 7,000,000 would leave."[77] Upon observing the Labor Day parade of 1936, Ball recorded in his diary that the African American workers under their union organization were "orderly, good-humored, apparently contented, happy."[78] Yet Ball's thoughts raced back from the 1930s to the gubernatorial election of 1876 between the Reconstruction candidate Daniel Chamberlain and the "Redeemer" Wade Hampton. With the election of 1876 still in question, black workers called "the Hunkidoris" traveled to Columbia to fight for Chamberlain should violence erupt.[79] The sight of organized black workers marching triggered this childhood recollection, and Ball immediately transferred that memory into a new set of fears: "I further reflected that these same negroes today, were they protected by soldiers and government, could in a few days or hours be converted by white scoundrels into the desperate and dangerous creatures that their grandfathers were. That is why I am an 'alarmist,' why I look with misgiving and apprehension upon the petting of the negroes by the national Democratic party."[80]

Ball recognized that the election of 1936 would prove important for Franklin Roosevelt. The first New Deal having had at best mixed results, Roosevelt faced a choice of either turning back toward the Right or plunging further to the Left. As the election neared, Ball wrote that "the sincere New Dealers, or 'Liberals' in congress, La Follette, Conyers, Nye, Bone, Norris will force the fighting. They will endeavor to erect a collectivist state, to enact state socialistic methods, to amend the constitution." Furthermore, their plans included "enforcement of the Fifteenth Amendment, the admission of negroes to political activity in the Democratic party in the South."[81]

Ball meanwhile anxiously awaited Roosevelt's second term and had ready his solution should Roosevelt make the fateful decision to turn again to the Left. Roosevelt did just that. Even before the votes were tallied, Ball began to dream of a new southern secession and, more realistically, a conservative southern bolt from the national Democratic Party. He wrote in July 1936, "Whether Roosevelt or Landon be elected, why should I care? . . . I have no party." [82] The swing of the African American vote to Roosevelt in the 1936 election confirmed in Ball's mind two fears—that Roosevelt was trying to "buy" votes through relief and that he in turn would use the power of the federal government to benefit his new allies. "Government from Washington," he groaned, "inevitably includes political equality of races." [83]

That there were prominent white southerners among the New Dealers offered Ball no comfort whatsoever. According to him, southern New Dealers "have abandoned the state sovereignty position solely from material considerations, for more offices, more money, more federal 'benefits'"; they had made the fatal mistake of following "the popular bent, almost without exception—and the popular bent, the mob disposition is now as always to fill guts with food and drink, avoid exertion and responsibility." [84] It certainly did not help his mood to consider that poor whites supported Franklin Roosevelt and the New Deal overwhelmingly. Not only did mill hands, for instance, support Roosevelt, but they understood that the federal government was now a potential ally in their struggle for better wages and working conditions. [85] By the late 1930s Ball maintained that he abhorred "any kind of 'contacts' with politicians and office-holders" of the day, since "they are nearly all low fellows." [86] At the core of the problem, Ball contended, was "the fact, that unlimited democracy is doomed to failure. The Roosevelt idea is universal suffrage and destruction of the power of the states." [87] To Bernard Baruch, Ball explained his version of South Carolina history. Reminding Baruch that "I am not a Democrat in a broad sense." Ball maintained that government was safe only in the hands of "a few sterling leaders." Even during the overthrow of Reconstruction in South Carolina, he added, "scores of excellent men of caliber and courage, too, needed the iron strength of Wade Hampton to keep them in straight courses." [88] Ball also kept in contact with the leading anti–New Deal southern Democrats. North Carolina congressman Josiah Bailey, author of the "Conservative Manifesto" of December 1937, wrote to Ball explaining that "we are making a battle for Constitutional Representative Government as opposed to mass democracy." [89]

Late in life Ball began to argue that the white South, outnumbered nationally and at odds with the Roosevelt-led New Deal, was being "forced" by the federal government to acknowledge the rights of African Americans. Black southerners renewed their struggle for the vote. In 1939 the new state conference of local NAACP chapters created a statewide network to help coordinate civil rights activity. In 1941 John McCray and Osceola McKaine arrived in Columbia, joining Modjeska Simkins and forming a relentless team of civil rights leaders within South Carolina.[90] Ball received reports of black South Carolinians applying to the University of South Carolina law school. These happenings were all part of the same threat, as far as Ball could see—the threat of democracy. To Fitzhugh McMaster, Ball wrote: "By what right . . . do those [who] profess to believe in 'democracy' . . . reject the negro? . . . Are not negroes American citizens? . . . Now I am not a democrat. I do not profess to believe in government by the people." Ball pushed his rhetoric to new heights—or depths—before signing off: and "in respect of the masses of the negroes I am a Fascist so far as the negroes are concerned. The fact is that in practice all Southern white men are Fascists so far as negroes are concerned."[91]

Others shared Ball's frantic side in the late 1930s and early 1940s. Ball received letters and updates on "The Bolshevik Conspiracy" and communist efforts among black southerners.[92] In 1943 Sen. Josiah W. Bailey of North Carolina wrote Ball that efforts to repeal the poll tax were not simply attacks on segregation but were the work of "men of the Communistic type." Bailey charged that the push for the poll tax repeal came not from "the Negroes so much as from that peculiar type of men in labor circles who became interested in the present war only after Russia was attacked by Germany." With no doubt unintentional irony, Bailey complained that labor leaders "have in mind a class government in which their leaders will rule."[93]

After the United States Supreme Court decision in *Smith v. Allwright* making white primaries illegal, Ball spoke before the Morris Brown A.M.E. Church in Charleston. He explained that his objection to "mixed primaries" was that "they would give us too much democracy." He added that this was not a racist position, since there was also "too much democracy in the white primary." Then moving beyond the issue of primaries and voting altogether, Ball concluded to his African American audience that "the ballot will never make you or any other people rich or independent, but soon or late independence, much the less riches, will give any people the ballot." After decades of arguing that African Americans should not and could not have the vote, Ball now argued that having the ballot would not make that much difference anyway.[94]

Black South Carolinians' political activism rattled Ball. In 1944 black Carolinians formed their own Progressive Democratic Party, and their candidate,

Osceola McKaine, ran against Olin D. Johnston for the U.S. Senate. McKaine had no delusions about winning; running and garnering votes, however many, gave further, concrete evidence of black political life. Despite widespread evidence of fraud and intimidation against McKaine voters, the state still tallied officially over three thousand votes for the Progressive Democratic Party candidate.[95]

The tide continued to run against Ball during these years. In 1947 federal judge J. Waties Waring rocked his fellow elite Charlestonians, and indeed much of South Carolina, by rejecting new all-white primary formats in *Elmore v. Rice.* In his ruling Judge Waring did not mince words, calling the state's contention that all-white primaries were the affairs of "private" political parties "pure sophistry." It was time, Judge Waring wrote, "for South Carolina to rejoin the Union." When the U.S. Supreme Court refused to hear the state's appeal in 1948, Waring's son-in-law Stanley Warren wrote the judge, "I can't wait to see what my pal Billy Ball has to say about it." [96]

For decades William Watts Ball had feared the day when white supremacy, elite and local rule, and the persuasive powers of South Carolina history and tradition would no longer work well enough to secure the conservatism he inherited and perpetuated. Ball, turning eighty years old, made his last stand for his conservatism in 1948. In February of that year his letter to the *New York Herald Tribune* established conservative themes mixing local rule and white supremacy. Ball held that the "'Negro question,' still acutely Southern, is passing and will pass out as a peculiar Southern affliction." Federal enforcement of civil rights for African Americans ultimately threatened "Wyoming, Maine, Iowa" as well as South Carolina because their rights as states would also be destroyed along the way. What options did a conservative such as Ball have? One was to hope that the 1948 election, with Henry Wallace already posing as a third candidate, ended up in the House of Representatives where conservative appeals to states' rights might take effect. Working in his usual attack on majoritarian rule, Ball explained that "the framers of the constitution had no purpose to create a democratic republic (note the small 'd'), nor were they thinking of 'two-party government,' now become a superstition which politicians preach to the populace." In a striking mixture of a conservative Old South definition of unionism with a nod to a very modern world, Ball concluded by adding: "This I have written as a believer in the Union—the Union of states, not necessarily of 143,000,000 people. It is written upon the assumption that fission of the atom does not presage destruction of our Republic, our Union, of states." [97]

Before the 1948 election season concluded, South Carolina once again stirred up national politics in fashion. At the state Democratic convention in January, Gov. J. Strom Thurmond warned that South Carolina's electoral votes would not go to Harry Truman, should the president be nominated at the national convention. True to his word, Thurmond, with Ball's full support, "bolted" the national Democratic Party; helped create a new States' Rights Democratic Party, the Dixiecrats; and found himself in the race for president. Ball celebrated by running an editorial in the *News and Courier* promoting "Thurmond for President." When the final election returns showed that the state's electoral votes indeed went to their Dixiecrat governor, Ball proclaimed that South Carolina was finally "free." [98]

The Party of our Fathers is Dead

Conservatives at Mid-Century

We want to know: what became of all those vital relationships and attitudes, and their corresponding modes of thought. . . . Did they merely sink into the past, or were they in some way conserved? If they were conserved, in what form have they been handed down to us?

—Karl Mannheim, "Conservative Thought"

In 1931, one year before publication of William Watts Ball's *The State That Forgot: South Carolina's Surrender to Democracy,* the Macmillan Company published *The Carolina Low-Country,* a collection of essays by members of Charleston's traditional elite families. Among the selections written by the Ravenels, Pinckneys, and Rutledges was DuBose Heyward's portrait of "The Negro in the Low-Country." Heyward, more famous for writing the novel that eventually became George and Ira Gershwin's *Porgy and Bess,* mixed an admission of slavery's faults with an affectionate memorial to its positive legacy.

Controlling the memory of slavery was a powerful tool in the postwar conservative's hands. Nearly always the lesson was that racial harmony came from racial hierarchy—meaning, of course, that racial harmony was guaranteed by white supremacy. Similar to Ball in *The State That Forgot,* Heyward noted that under a good master "a bond of friendship and sympathetic understanding" developed with the slave. Heyward conceded that the image of the contented slave had been "sentimentalized and utilized *ad nauseam.*" This could not, however, "obliterate the fact" that in the master/slave relationship there was "something beautiful and tender and enriching to both black and white."[1]

Just two years earlier DuBose Heyward's fictionalized account of life in Charleston during the early 1900s, *Mamba's Daughters,* was published. In that book St. Julien de Chatigny Wentworth, an eighteen-year-old from an aristocratic ancestry, considered his first employment. "Unfortunately," Heyward narrated, "there were only certain occupations that a gentleman could follow in Charleston without sacrifice of family dignity," and these usually required professional training that "Saint" lacked. The lowcountry experienced a brief boom in phosphate mining in the late 1800s and early 1900s, and Saint, growing discouraged, finally went to see the local owner of a phosphate mine. "Fertilizers!" he scoffed inwardly. "This was about the end of the procession; the last stand." As his interview proceeded, Saint daydreamed about the chance to show his worth to both his employer and the miners. "Perhaps there would be a riot" and he could save the day, left alone "reasoning with the mob." The implication in Saint's fantasy was that mobs, inclined toward being unreasonable, would respond to a Wentworth's status in the community and place in history.[2]

That both themes—white rule over black and elite control over all— should appear in Heyward's writing is not surprising. Conservatives in South Carolina still believed that history demanded that society be arranged along these lines. They were especially inclined to see life in the postslavery South as one under siege by "the masses" and "mobs." From Frederick A. Porcher to William Watts Ball, conservatives observed to their satisfaction that "mobs"—black and white—went on strike; voted for bad, ignorant people; and in general misbehaved with irritating frequency. DuBose Heyward's fiction frequently evoked traditional conservative ideals. One would do well, however, to recall Fritz Stern's observation of German conservatives during the same years: "Everything beginning in mystique ended in politics."[3] Three of the four individuals discussed in this study held public office, and the fourth, William Watts Ball, was perhaps more influential politically than the other three. They all wrote candidly of their thoughts and acted accordingly, as well as publicly. All knew that their words and deeds contained important political implications.

At one level a comparative look at conservative positions taken in the 1850s and those of the early 1900s appear to produce no consistency. In the last decade before the Civil War, Frederick A. Porcher developed his defense of slavery as an institution that organized society safely, rejecting in his prewar writings bourgeois liberalism. Theodore D. Jervey Jr.'s work during the decades around the new century used fiction and progressive-era-style, "scientific" research to raise questions about segregation at its inception. He praised the free-market system for alleviating South Carolina's "negro problem" through migration. During the 1920s and 1930s, however, William Watts Ball, grew angry at "big business" and clung ferociously to segregation as a matter of social control against both race and class unrest caused by the Great Depression.

But with and without slaves, through the fall of the old plantation system and the rise of the cotton mill, at the peak of the laissez-faire years of the Gilded Age and against the full centralizing force of the New Deal, South Carolina's conservatives believed that history proved beyond doubt that a local elite should rule a decentralized political system and that the white "race" was superior. When the New Deal became a fixed reality, and not a wide-ranging set of emergency solutions, South Carolina's conservatives feared the worse. In 1936 William Watts Ball, thinking about the impending reelection of Franklin Roosevelt, wrote dejectedly, "I have no party."[4] He was right. By 1945 more southern conservatives arrived at the same conclusion, and in 1948 South Carolina's J. Strom Thurmond emerged as the nominee for the States' Rights Democratic Party.

Most would assume that the Dixiecrat movement of white southerners out of the national Democratic Party came in response to the Truman administration's intimations that it would enforce civil rights for African Americans. This is partly correct. Certainly African Americans had made significant gains in their freedom struggle. The court cases of *Smith v. Allwright, Elmore v. Rice,* and *Brown v. Boskins* dismantled the white primaries and sparked voter registration drives in South Carolina. The Truman administration released *To Secure These Rights,* calling for the end of racial discrimination. African American veterans returned from war more determined than ever to challenge segregation. But from William Watts Ball's perspective in 1936, preserving segregation was far from his sole worry. When Ball declared that he had "no party," he also felt threatened and disgusted by the willingness of poor white South Carolinians to turn to the federal government for relief and protection. Bryant Simon's *A Fabric of Defeat* includes in its analysis the letters written by white mill hands in support of New Deal efforts on behalf of workers. That white South Carolina workers now urged "Mr. Roosevelt" to "use the big stick" against textile-mill owners—that when perceived as having been dealt with unfairly mill hands responded defiantly, "Mr. Roosevelt ain't going to stand for this"—signaled bad tidings for a conservative such as Ball.[5]

Ball's conservatism, having been passed along from, for example, Frederick Porcher and Edward McCrady, stands midway between Theodore G. Barker's in November 1860 and Strom Thurmond's in 1964. Barker chastised northern society, about to be governed by the Republican Party of Abraham Lincoln, as the home of ignorant voters, greedy businessmen, and unruly working masses: "See their forms of Democracy driving onward to the licence of mob-law, and their Conservatism quailing before the tyranny of mere numbers. See Capital hurrying home in gilded chariots, with curtains drawn, to hide its head in innermost retreats from the ferocious demands and threats of hungry labor." Barker invoked the memory of George Washington in the South's looming "battle for freedom and for Constitutional Government." [6]

Strom Thurmond characterized the election of 1964 as one in which "the future of freedom and constitutional government is at stake." Thurmond's conservatism was not exactly the same as William Watts Ball's. Growing up in an Edgefield household that hosted Ben Tillman as a frequent guest, Thurmond could not and did not share Ball's elitism. Gone were the open criticism of, as Ball liked to put it, small "d" democracy. But Ball, who died in 1952, and Barker would have likely approved of important parts of Thurmond's 1964 speech. Like Barker in 1860, Thurmond proclaimed that the ruling party, now the Democrats under Lyndon Johnson, did the bidding of "minority groups, power-hungry union leaders . . . and big businessmen." As the ruling party, the Democrats, he continued "encouraged lawlessness, civil unrest and mob actions." The party, Thurmond charged, "worships at the throne of power and materialism," all at the expense of the "spiritual values and political principles which have brought us the blessings of freedom." This was not, Thurmond explained, the Democratic Party of his ancestors, and he lamented that "the party of our fathers is dead." Since "the future of freedom and constitutional government are at stake," Thurmond found no choice but to leave the party and pledge his support for the Republican Party and its nominee Barry Goldwater. South Carolina's conservatives were on the move yet again. [7]

Notes

Introduction

1. Alexis de Tocqueville, *The Old Regime and the French Revolution* (New York: Harper & Brothers, 1856).

2. W. J. Cash, *The Mind of the South* (New York: A. A. Knopf, 1941), 1.

3. Katharine Du Pre Lumpkin, *The Making of a Southerner* (Athens: University of Georgia Press, 1981), 235–37.

4. Quoted in Manisha Sinha, *The Counterrevolution of Slavery: Politics and Ideology in Antebellum South Carolina* (Chapel Hill: University of North Carolina Press, 2000), 140.

5. Arno Mayer, *The Persistence of the Old Regime: Europe to the Great War* (New York: Pantheon Books, 1981), 4.

6. W. D. Porter, *College and Collegians. An Address Delivered by W. D. Porter, before the Alumni Association of the College of Charleston, on Commencement Day, 28th March, 1871* (Charleston, S.C.: Walker, Evans, & Cogswell, Printers and Stationers, 1871), 5.

7. *Sermons by the Right Reverend Stephen Elliott, D.D., Late Bishop of Georgia. With a Memoir, by Thomas M. Hanckel, Esq.* (New York: Pott and Amery, 1867), xv–xvi.

8. William J. Rivers, *Address Delivered before the South Carolina Historical Society on Their Twenty-First Anniversary, May 19, 1876* (Charleston, S.C.: The News and Courier Job Presses, 1876), 24.

9. Charles E. Cauthen, ed., *Family Letters of the Three Wade Hamptons, 1782–1901* (Columbia: University of South Carolina Press, 1953), 142–43.

10. Charles J. Holden, "Is Our Love for Wade Hampton Foolishness?: South Carolina and the Lost Cause," in *The Myth of the Lost Cause and Civil War History,* edited by Gary W. Gallagher and Alan T. Nolan (Bloomington: Indiana University Press, 2000).

11. William J. Cooper Jr., *The Conservative Regime: South Carolina, 1877–1890* (Baton Rouge: Louisiana State University Press, 1968), 207.

12. Walter B. Edgar, *South Carolina: A History* (Columbia: University of South Carolina Press, 1998), 383, 407.

13. Richard M. Weaver's *The Southern Tradition at Bay: A History of Postbellum Thought,* edited by George Core and M. E. Bradford (New Rochelle, N.Y.: Arlington House, 1968; reprint, Washington, D.C.: Regnery Gateway, 1989), is a notable exception to this assertion.

14. Russell Kirk, *The Conservative Mind: From Burke to Eliot,* 7th rev. ed. (Washington, D.C.: Regnery Publishing Inc., 1994), 338.

15. M. E. Bradford, "The Lasting Lesson of Southern Politics," in M. E. Bradford, *Remembering Who We Are: Observations of a Southern Conservative* (Athens: University of Georgia Press, 1985), 57–60.

16. Lacy Ford, in *Origins of Southern Radicalism, 1800–1860* (Oxford and New York: Oxford University Press, 1988), argues that white male suffrage created a shared commitment by elites and nonelites to a republican vision and discourse for South Carolina. More recently, Minisha Sinha's *Counterrevolution of Slavery* examines the power the slave-owning elite maintained despite the state's image as a herrenvolk democracy. The enormous amount of antidemocratic sentiments and activity by the state's elites, she argues, undermines Ford's republican thesis for antebellum South Carolina.

17. George Brown Tindall, *The Persistent Tradition in New South Politics* (Baton Rouge: Louisiana State University Press, 1975), xii, 19, 20–21.

18. Vilfredo Pareto, *The Mind and Society: A Treatise on General Sociology* (New York: Harcourt, Bruce, and Company, Inc., 1935), 3:1431.

19. Jaroslav Pelikan's *The Vindication of Tradition* (New Haven and London: Yale University Press, 1984) offers valuable insights into the origins, meanings, and workings of tradition. Pelikan argues that the attention devoted to the historicism of tradition has obscured the substance that remains.

20. Allen Tate, "Remarks on Southern Religion," in Twelve Southerners, *I'll Take My Stand: The South and the Agrarian Tradition* (Baton Rouge: Louisiana State University Press, 1930), 155.

21. Pelikan, *Vindication of Tradition,* 51.

22. Elizabeth Fox-Genovese, "The Anxiety of History: The Southern Confrontation with Modernity," *Southern Cultures* (inaugural issue 1993): 77.

23. Ben Robertson, *Red Hills and Cotton: An Upcountry Memory* (New York: A. A. Knopf, 1942), 28.

24. William A. Percy, *Lanterns on the Levee: Recollections of a Planter's Son* (New York: A. A. Knopf, 1941), 229.

25. See, for example, Lewis P. Simpson, "The Southern Recovery of Memory and History," *The Sewanee Review* 45 (1974): 1–32.

26. Tindall, *Persistent Tradition in New South Politics,* 2.

27. Frederick A. Porcher, "Memoirs of Frederick Augustus Porcher," *South Carolina Historical Magazine* (hereafter abbreviated as *SCHM*) 45 (1944): 66.

28. Frederick A. Porcher, "The Conflict of Capital and Labor," *Russell's Magazine* 3 (1858): 289.

29. Edward McCrady, *Registration of Electors*, South Caroliniana Library, University of South Carolina, Columbia, 11.

30. Robertson, *Red Hills and Cotton,* 100.

31. William Watts Ball Diary, vol. 4, 11 Nov. 1918, 238, William Watts Ball Papers, Special Collections, Perkins Library, Duke University, Durham, N.C.

32. Ball to C. L. Cobb, 9 Nov. 1933, William Watts Ball Papers.

Chapter One

1. Porcher, "Memoirs," *SCHM* 47 (1946): 83; Frederick A. Porcher, *An Oration Delivered before the Inhabitants of Pineville, So. Ca. on Monday, July 4th, 1831, the 56th Anniversary of the Declaration of Independence,* edited by Samuel Gaillard Stoney (Charleston, S.C.: J. W. Burges, 1831), 5.

2. Porcher, *Oration Delivered before the Inhabitants of Pineville,* 3–6.

3. Porcher, "Memoirs," *SCHM* 47 (1946): 83.

4. The information in this paragraph is also taken from Porcher's memoirs, which, he indicates, he wrote shortly after the Civil War. The complete listing of his memoirs are in the bibliography. See also Michael O'Brien, ed., *All Clever Men Who Make Their Way: Critical Discourse in the Old South* (Fayetteville: University of Arkansas Press, 1982), 312–36.

5. Porcher, *Oration,* 5, 8.

6. Ibid., 7, 14–15. The rationalism behind the American Revolution set it apart in Porcher's mind from the other notable revolution of the late 1700s, the French Revolution. The French Revolution had been a "brilliant spectacle" but, not surprisingly, suffered from "little reflection" and was thus "easily diverted into any current by the intrigues of designing demagogues . . . ending at last in military despotism" (7).

7. Ibid., 14–15. For insight into the influence of the nullification crisis, see Sinha, *Counterrevolution of Slavery,* especially chapters 1 and 2; William Freehling, *Prelude to Civil War: The Nullification Controversy in South Carolina, 1816–1836* (New York: Harper and Row, 1966); and Ford, *Origins of Southern Radicalism.*

8. Porcher, "Memoirs," *SCHM* 47 (1946): 81–92; (1946): 140–58; 48 (1947): 108; (1946): 205–8.

9. For discussion of South Carolina's economic difficulties during these years, see Lacy Ford's *Origins of Southern Radicalism* and Freehling's *Prelude to Civil War.*

10. Despite the career change, on the eve of the Civil War, Porcher still owned at least twelve slaves while living in Charleston. See "Slave Inhabitants in the City

of Charleston," United States Census, 1860, Charleston County, South Carolina, Slave Schedules, reel 4, p. 14, Charleston County Library, Charleston, S.C.

11. Drew Gilpin Faust, *A Sacred Circle: The Dilemma of the Intellectual in the Old South, 1840–1860* (Philadelphia: University of Pennsylvania Press, 1986), 10.

12. "As everything in this country depends upon favor and influence," Porcher noted later, "I had reasonable hopes of being the professor." Porcher had a brother-in-law among the college's board of trustees as well as "other friends." The president of the college was Peronneau Finley, a relative of Porcher's late wife. See Porcher, "Memoirs," *SCHM* 48 (1947): 107, 152.

13. For the best work on the proslavery ideology, see Eugene Genovese, *The Slave-holder's Dilemma: Freedom and Progress in Southern Conservative Thought, 1820–1860* (Columbia: University of South Carolina Press, 1992); Faust, *Sacred Circle* (Philadelphia: University of Pennsylvania Press, 1986); Harvey Wish, *George Fitzhugh: Propagandist of the Old South* (Baton Rouge: Louisiana State University Press, 1943); Elizabeth Fox-Genovese, *Within the Plantation Household: Black and White Women of the Old South* (Chapel Hill and London: University of North Carolina Press, 1988); Ford, *Origins of Southern Radicalism*; and most recently, Sinha, *Counterrevolution of Slavery*.

14. Fox-Genovese, *Within the Plantation Household.*

15. Frederick A. Porcher, "The Nature and Claims of Paradox," *Russell's Magazine* 1 (1857): 485.

16. Frederick A. Porcher, "False Views of History," *Southern Quarterly Review* n.s. 6 (1852): 31–32.

17. Ibid., 33.

18. Ibid., 33, 34.

19. Ibid., 34, 35.

20. Ibid., 42, 44. Porcher's source for information on Philip II and the Inquisition was a history of the Inquisition by a Rev. Jayme Balmes, a Spanish priest; see Peter Linehan, *History and Historians of Medieval Spain* (New York: Oxford University Press, 1993). Demonstrating his familiarity with the most recent thought and method in history, Porcher cited a more famous historian, Leopold von Ranke, whose assessment of Philip was similar to Balmes's. Von Ranke, according to Porcher, had "no prejudices of either religion or politics, to induce him to defend the character of Philip" (Porcher, "False Views of History," 45).

21. Frederick A. Porcher, "Bancroft's History of the United States," *Russell's Magazine* 3 (1858): 521.

22. Ibid.

23. Ibid., 521, 524. Porcher wryly noted that John Wesley, the founder of Method-ism, received much different treatment at Bancroft's hands: "He touches Wesley with the tenderest charity. Whence this difference?" Porcher suspected that the difference had to do with Bancroft's consciousness of his reading (and purchas-ing) audience: "Mr. Bancroft is careful not to offend the Methodists by any cen-sure of their founder . . . Johnson may be lashed with impunity. . . . But Wesley—the Methodists are a powerful body" (524).

24. Ibid., 525. With this redefinition of independence, not revolution, Porcher aligned himself with the more prominent South Carolina historian William Henry Trescot. Porcher's revision shows the shifting interpretation of indepen-dence that many conservative South Carolinians held as their slave society was increasingly on the defensive.

25. Frederick A. Porcher, *Eulogy on the Late Hon. John C. Calhoun, Delivered before the Cliosophic and Chrestomathic Societies of the College of Charleston, on Thursday, June 6th, 1850* (Charleston, S.C.: John Russell, 1850), 7.

26. Frederick A. Porcher, "Address Pronounced at the Inauguration of the South Carolina Historical Society, June 28, 1857, by F. A. Porcher," in *Collections of the South Carolina Historical Society,* vol. 1 (Charleston, S.C.: S. G. Courtenay and Company, 1857), 2. Porcher's definition of republicanism as family based and historically grounded was also in stark contrast to increasingly powerful free-labor definitions, as he no doubt was aware. Stephanie McCurry's *Masters of Small Worlds: Yeoman Households, Gender Relations, and the Political Culture of the Antebellum South Carolina Low Country* (Oxford, London, and New York: Oxford University Press, 1995) offers a close and thoroughly researched look at social and political power through the values of a hierarchical family structure. Both Eric Foner in *Free Soil, Free Labor, Free Men: The Ideology of the Republican Party before the Civil War* (Oxford, London, and New York: Oxford University Press, 1970) and Julie Saville's introduction to her *The Work of Reconstruction: From Slave to Wage Laborer in South Carolina, 1860–1870* (New York and Cambridge: Cambridge University Press, 1994) demonstrate the contrast with free-labor republicanism as based more on economic opportunity for a nation of small independent owner-producers.

27. Porcher, "Address," 2.

28. Ibid., 8–9.

29. Genovese, *Slaveholder's Dilemma,* 20.

30. Frederick A. Porcher, "Southern and Northern Civilizations Contrasted," *Russell's Magazine* 1 (1857): 102. Here Porcher shares a view close to Simms's experience

of "growing more & more suspicious" of the reliance on rational thought at the heart of mid-nineteenth-century views of progress (quoted in Faust, *Sacred Circle,* 50). He also struck a chord similar to that of William Porcher Miles, a fellow College of Charleston faculty member, later a Confederate congressman, and finally president of South Carolina College; Miles in 1849 spoke out in frustration with "this utilitarian age" (quoted in Eric Walther, *The Fire-Eaters* [Baton Rouge and London: Louisiana State University Press, 1992], 275).

31. Porcher, "Nature and Claims of Paradox," 481; Porcher, "Conflict of Capital and Labor," 289.

32. Porcher, "Conflict of Capital and Labor," 289.

33. James Henry Hammond, "Letter to an English Abolitionist," reprinted in *The Ideology of Slavery: Proslavery Thought in the Antebellum South, 1830–1860,* edited by Drew Gilpin Faust (Baton Rouge and London: Louisiana State University Press, 1981), 177.

34. Porcher, "Conflict of Capital and Labor," 290.

35. Genovese, *Slaveholders' Dilemma,* 3–8.

36. Porcher, "Conflict of Capital and Labor," 290.

37. Ibid., 295–96. Porcher chose his topic, Scottish enclosure movements, well. Through acts of Parliament, Scottish landowners were given more flexibility to effect changes in land use and tenure than were their English counterparts. Thus, according to S. G. E. Lythe and J. Butt, enclosure in Scotland "largely depended upon market considerations and long term trends in price" (*An Economic History of Scotland, 1100–1939* [Glasgow and London: Blackie and Son, Limited, 1975], 109–10).

38. Porcher, "Conflict of Labor and Capital," 295–96.

39. Porcher, "Nature and Claims of Paradox," 488. Similarly, fellow South Carolinian William F. Hutson asked of the times, "To the rich, have been added comforts, and appliances unknown to their fathers; but are the mass better fed?—better clothed?—happier?—more contented?—even freer?" (William F. Hutson, "The History of the Girondists, or Personal Memoirs of the Patriots of the French Revolution," *Southern Presbyterian Review* 2 [1848]: 398; also quoted in Genovese, *Slaveholders' Dilemma,* 29).

40. Porcher, "Nature and Claims of Paradox," 485.

41. Porcher, "Conflict of Capital and Labor," 289.

42. Porcher, *Oration,* 8; "Nature and Claims of Paradox," 486.

43. Porcher, "Southern and Northern Civilizations," 104.

44. Porcher, "Nature and Claims of Paradox," 486–87.

45. From J. M. Robson, *John Stuart Mill: A Selection of His Works* (New York: St. Martin's Press, 1966), 324. Even though much of Porcher's critique on the industrialization of England and the implications for the poor echoes Mill's, it is perhaps not surprising that he found this passage in Mill's *Principles* unacceptable. Critiques aside, they differed sharply on matters of social organization. Mill used a historical argument to ridicule those, such as Porcher, who believed that all of society was better off under the rule and care of a traditional ruling elite. "It has never been historically realized," Mill wrote. "It makes its appeal to our imaginative sympathies in the character of a restoration of the good times of our forefathers. But no times can be pointed out in which the higher classes of this or any other country performed a part even distantly resembling the one assigned to them in this theory" (331).

46. Porcher, "Conflict of Capital and Labor," 296.

47. Ibid., 297. Carlyle discussed both universal education and emigration in his chapter titled "Impossible" in *Chartism*, published in 1839.

48. Porcher, "False Views of History," 39–40.

49. Porcher, "Conflict of Capital and Labor," 297.

50. Ibid., 294, 297.

51. Porcher, "Southern and Northern Civilizations," 98.

52. Porcher, "Conflict of Capital and Labor," 290.

53. Porcher, "Southern and Northern Civilizations," 101.

54. Fox-Genovese, "Anxiety of History," 73.

55. Frederick A. Porcher, "Webster's Dictionary," *Russell's Magazine* 5 (1859): 419.

56. Porcher, "Southern and Northern Civilizations," 103.

57. Porcher, "Conflict of Capital and Labor," 293.

58. Porcher, "Southern and Northern Civilizations," 107.

59. Porcher, *Eulogy on the Late Hon. John C. Calhoun*, 20.

60. Porcher, "False Views of History," 48.

61. Porcher, "Nature and Claims of Paradox," 487.

Chapter 2

1. Frederick A. Porcher, "The Last Chapter in the History of Reconstruction in South Carolina," *Southern Historical Society Papers* (hereafter abbreviated as *SHSP*) 13 (1885): 81. Porcher's sentiments were not uncommon among the Old South's elite. Princeton graduate and former Confederate officer George Anderson Mercer wrote after the war, "I have no country, no flag, no emblems, no public

spirit," while diarist Cornelia Phillips Spencer added, "I do not love my country. I feel rather as if I had no country" (both quoted in Clement Eaton, *The Waning of the Old South Civilization, 1860–1880s* [Athens: University of Georgia Press, 1968], 118, 113).

2. Frederick A. Porcher to Judah P. Benjamin, 16 Dec. 1864, John T. Picketts Papers, microfilm copy in the Alderman Library, University of Virginia, Charlottesville.

3. Clelia Porcher to "Dear Sister," 9 May 1865, Frederick A. Porcher Papers, folder 1, South Caroliniana Library, University of South Carolina, Columbia.

4. Drew Gilpin Faust captures the relationship between slave ownership and local power in a straightforward description: "A master's power had necessarily to be forged at home, but it then stretched well beyond the immediate boundaries of his plantation; effective dominance over land and slaves led naturally to authority over other whites in the immediate locality and could even reach throughout the state and the nation at large" (Drew Gilpin Faust, *James Henry Hammond and the Old South: A Design for Mastery* [Baton Rouge and London: Louisiana State University Press, 1982], 131).

5. Sinha, *Counterrevolution of Slavery*; Charles B. Dew, *Apostles of Disunion: Southern Secession Commissioners and the Causes of the Civil War* (Charlottesville and London: University of Virginia Press, 2001).

6. Pierre Manent in *An Intellectual History of Liberalism* (Princeton, N.J.: Princeton University Press, 1994) notes among liberal theorists in the 1800s an increasing consciousness of living under the "authority of history" and not simply in the midst of it (81–82). Porcher's acceptance of this notion is in stark contrast to his youthful views of 1831 when through their ability to think for themselves Americans had broken from a past that was all "gloom and darkness" and announced "the dawn of a day that will have no end."

7. Weaver, *Southern Tradition at Bay*, 96–160.

8. Saville, *Work of Reconstruction*, 8–11.

9. Bernard E. Powers Jr., "Community Evolution and Race Relations in Reconstruction Charleston," *South Carolina Historical Magazine* 95 (1994): 27–28.

10. "Conservative Convention," *Charleston Daily Courier*, 9 Nov. 1867, 1.

11. Porcher, *Eulogy on the Late Hon. John C. Calhoun*, 6.

12. Porcher, "Memoirs," *SCHM* 47 (1946): 203.

13. "Conservative Convention," *Charleston Daily Courier*, 9 Nov. 1867, 1.

14. Ibid.

15. Both are quoted in Lacy K. Ford Jr., "Republics and Democracy," in *The Meaning of South Carolina History: Essays in Honor of George C. Rogers, Jr.* (Columbia: University of South Carolina Press, 1991), 132–33.

16. "Conservative Convention," *Charleston Daily Courier,* 9 Nov. 1867, 1.

17. In his biography on George Fitzhugh, an extreme proslavery writer of the 1850s, Harvey Wish notes that to a large extent following the war "the Virginian's hatred of the capitalistic spirit had disappeared." Fitzhugh, like Porcher, maintained his belief in natural hierarchy. He now was confident that free-labor competition would create the same stratification, particularly racial, if allowed to operate without state interference. Fitzhugh, however, went so far as to condone the "natural" formation of monopolies as establishing order and "sustaining . . . civilization." See Wish, *George Fitzhugh,* 337.

18. Frederick A. Porcher, lecture entitled "Charleston—City of Planters," Porcher Papers, Special Collections, Robert Scott Small Library, College of Charleston, Charleston, S.C. Few expressed this view as plainly as the economist and later president of Yale University Arthur Twining Hadley, who wrote, "The danger of believing that economic laws can be interfered with by human effort is ten times greater than the danger of an extreme belief in laissez faire" (quoted in Sidney Fine, *Laissez Faire and the General-Welfare State: A Study of Conflict in American Thought, 1865–1901* [Ann Arbor: University of Michigan Press, 1956], 56).

19. Porcher, "Memoirs," *SCHM* 48 (1947): 83.

20. Ibid., 95–96. Porcher did eventually contribute some French translations to *Magnolia* and later wrote a number of articles used in the earlier chapter for Simms's journal *Russell's Magazine.* Porcher acknowledged Simms's influence in an 1855 letter stating, "I have lived an idle person all my life, dreaming on the plantation, and have hardly written a line but at your suggestion" (Mary Simms Oliphant, Alfred Taylor Odell, and T. C. Duncan Eaves, eds., *The Letters of William Gilmore Simms* [Columbia: University of South Carolina Press, 1953], 2:567, 213 n).

21. Porcher, "Memoirs," *SCHM* 49 (1948): 25.

22. "Charleston—City of Planters," Porcher Papers, Special Collections, Robert Scott Small Library, College of Charleston, Charleston, S.C.

23. Porcher, *Eulogy on the Late Hon. John C. Calhoun,* 6.

24. "Charleston—City of Planters," Porcher Papers, Special Collections, Robert Scott Small Library, College of Charleston, Charleston, S.C. François Furet found a similar approach in one of Porcher's favorite historians, Edward Gibbon. Gibbon, Furet notes, wrote "moral history." Therefore, according to Furet's reading of Gibbon, instead of political or military success, "for a period to be great, it was necessary, but also sufficient, for it to have produced a certain kind of men" (François Furet, "Civilization and Barbarism in Gibbon's History," in *Edmund Gibbon and the Decline and Fall of the Roman Empire,* edited by

G. W. Bowersock, John Clive, and Stephen R. Graubard (Cambridge and London: Harvard University Press, 1977), 161.

25. Porcher, "Address," 2.

26. Porcher, "Memoirs," *SCHM* 45 (1944): 80.

27. Ibid., 67.

28. Ibid., 45 (1944): 141–42.

29. Ibid., 49 (1948): 20–23.

30. Thomas Holt, *Black Over White: Negro Political Leadership in South Carolina during Reconstruction* (Urbana and Chicago: University of Illinois Press, 1977), 1, 95.

31. "Origins of Language as Taught by the Philosophers of the Eighteenth Century," Porcher Papers, Special Collections, Robert Scott Small Library, College of Charleston, Charleston, S.C. An 1875 appointment of an African American to a local judicial position prompted the *Charleston News and Courier* to run the headline "CIVILIZATION IN PERIL" (quoted in Holt, *Black Over White,* 95).

32. From an untitled postwar lecture by Porcher on antebellum history beginning with "While I was preparing the two former lectures," Porcher Papers, box 3, folder 2, Special Collections, Robert Scott Small Library, College of Charleston, Charleston, S.C. For valuable accounts of the transition from slave to free South Carolina, see Joel Williamson, *After Slavery: The Negro in South Carolina during Reconstruction, 1865–1877* (Chapel Hill: University of North Carolina Press, 1965); Willie Lee Rose, *Rehearsal for Reconstruction: The Port Royal Experiment* (New York: Oxford University Press, 1965); George Brown Tindall, *South Carolina Negroes, 1877–1900* (Columbia: University of South Carolina Press, 1952); and Cooper, *Conservative Regime.*

33. Holt, *Black Over White,* 100–101.

34. Saville, *Work of Reconstruction,* 59–62, 99–101, 177–82.

35. Porcher, "Last Chapter in the History of Reconstruction," 556.

36. Porcher, lecture beginning "While I was preparing two former lectures."

37. Frederick George Porcher to Caroline Porcher, 16 Oct. 1864, Frederick A. Porcher Papers, South Carolina Historical Society, Charleston.

38. John Berkeley Grimball Diary, 20 Mar. 1862, Southern Historical Collection, University of North Carolina, Chapel Hill.

39. Porcher, lecture beginning with "While I was preparing the two former lectures."

40. Anne Porcher to "My dear Mary," 12 Sept. 1876, Frederick A. Porcher Papers, South Caroliniana Library, University of South Carolina, Columbia.

41. Weaver, *Southern Tradition at Bay,* 158.

42. Frederick A. Porcher, lecture entitled "A Brief of Guizot's Essay on Representative Government in England," Porcher Papers, Special Collections, Robert

Scott Small Library, College of Charleston, Charleston, S.C., 13. This same issue produced decades of tension between traditional elite South Carolinians and their more rural, democratically inclined fellow white citizens; see Ford, *Origins of Southern Radicalism.*

43. Frederick A. Porcher, lecture entitled "On Different Forms of Government and Their Value," Porcher Papers, College of Charleston, Charleston, S.C., 17.

44. Frederick A. Porcher, *Governor Rutledge. The Attacks of a Brooklyn Editor Vigorously Repelled. A Masterly Review of the Great South Carolinian's Character,* Wilson Library Pamphlets Collection, University of North Carolina, Chapel Hill.

45. Frederick A. Porcher, lecture entitled "Introductory Lecture," Porcher Papers, Special Collections, Robert Scott Small Library, College of Charleston, Charleston, S.C., 8–9.

46. Frederick A. Porcher, lecture entitled "Political and Social Troubles," Porcher Papers, Special Collections, Robert Scott Small Library, College of Charleston, Charleston, S.C., 9.

47. Porcher, "On Different Forms of Government and Their Value," Porcher Papers, College of Charleston, Charleston, S.C., 5. Other antebellum conservatives disdained the U.S. Constitution on different grounds. Preston Brooks, peeved that the Free Soil movement seemed to be making political headway, recommended that his fellow southerners "tear the Constitution of the United States, trample it underfoot, and form a Southern Confederacy, every state of which will be a slaveholding state" (Sinha, *Counterrevolution of Slavery,* 189).

48. Frederick A. Porcher to Judah P. Benjamin, 16 Dec. 1864, John T. Picketts Papers, microfilm copy in Alderman Library, University of Virginia, Charlottesville.

49. Porcher, "On Different Forms of Government and Their Value," Porcher Papers, College of Charleston, Charleston, S.C., 7, 5–10. Relying on his traditional white southern understanding of this "spirit under which the people have grown and lived," Porcher therefore did not know whether old abolitionists such as Charles Sumner were ignorant or spiteful in insisting that border states Maryland and Kentucky rewrite their constitutions to include black suffrage.

50. Ibid., 10–11.

51. Ibid., 18–19.

52. Porcher, "Political and Social Troubles," Porcher Papers, College of Charleston, Charleston, S.C., 4, 5.

53. Ibid., 5–6. See also Eric Foner, *Nothing but Freedom: Emancipation and Its Legacy* (Baton Rouge and London: Louisiana State University, 1983), 50. Immediately after the war South Carolina's planters similarly sought to use government

to control labor costs and mobility. There is no direct evidence that Porcher intended his criticism of English landowners to apply to South Carolina planters, however.

54. Porcher, "Political and Social Troubles," 6, 7–9, 15–16.

55. Frederick A. Porcher to Caroline Smith Parker, 23 Sept. 1875, Porcher Papers, South Caroliniana Library, University of South Carolina, Columbia.

56. Porcher, "Political and Social Troubles," 11–12.

57. Ibid., 12.

58. Porcher, "Political and Social Troubles," 12–13. Porcher did understand to a certain extent labor's frustrations. In this same lecture he referred to the railroad strikes of 1876, noting that "last year when the middle states were distracted by Rail Road riots, it was ascertained that one of the most powerful of the Railway corporations had made large inroads upon the wages of its workmen, while it continued to pay its shareholders the enormous interest of 10 per cent." He continued disapprovingly, "Here was greed exhibited in a most glaring manner. . . . It is not surprising that a spirit of revenge seized the sufferers."

59. See, for instance, *Charleston Daily Courier,* 8 Jan. 1867.

60. Frederick A. Porcher to Caroline Smith Parker, 25 Sept. 1875, Porcher Papers, South Caroliniana Library, University of South Carolina, Columbia.

61. Porcher, "Last Chapter in the History of Reconstruction," 241–42. For a good discussion of the 1876 rice workers' strike, see Foner's *Nothing but Freedom.*

62. Porcher, "Last Chapter in the History of Reconstruction," 241–42.

63. Ibid., 243.

64. Ibid.

Chapter 3

1. "Slave Inhabitants in Christ Church," *1860 Census, Charleston County, South Carolina, Slave Schedules,* reel 4, p. 9, Charleston County Library, Charleston, S.C.

2. *Confederate Military History Extended Version* (Wilmington, N.C.: Broadfoot Publishing Company, 1987), 721–22.

3. Ibid., 722; *Charleston News and Courier,* 2 Nov. 1903; Dumas Malone, ed., *Dictionary of American Biography,* vol. 12 (New York: Charles Scribner's Sons, 1933), 1–2.

4. Edward McCrady Jr. to Edward McCrady L'Engle, 28 Mar. 1866, Edward McCrady L'Engle Papers, Southern Historical Collection, University of North Carolina, Chapel Hill.

5. Edward McCrady Jr. to Edward McCrady L'Engle, 19 Dec. 1866, Edward McCrady L'Engle Papers, Southern Historical Collection, University of North Carolina, Chapel Hill.

6. Edward McCrady Jr., *A Review of the Resolutions of the Press Conference* (Charleston, S.C.: Walker, Evans, & Cogswell, 1870), 12–13.

7. McCrady's conservative principles focused primarily on the state of politics in South Carolina. There is no evidence he wrestled with the economic direction South Carolina took with the destruction of slavery in the way Frederick Porcher did. His personal papers indicate that in the postwar years he became the largest stockholder in a venture called the Valley River Mining Company. See the Edward McCrady, Jr. Papers, Legal Papers, South Carolina Historical Society, Charleston.

8. McCrady Jr., *A Review of the Resolutions,* 12–13.

9. Oliphant, Odell, and Eaves, eds., *Letters of William Gilmore Simms,* 5:306.

10. Hanckel, *Sermons by the Right Reverend Stephen Elliott,* xv–xvi.

11. Thomas M. Hanckel, "South Carolina—Her State Sovereignty," *De Bow's Review* 29 (20 Sept. 1860): 315. In the early 1850s Kossuth toured the United States on behalf of Hungarian independence. In a speech delivered in Boston he proclaimed that "liberty is a principle; its community is its security; exclusiveness is its doom. What is aristocracy? It is exclusive liberty; it is privilege; and aristocracy is doomed, because it is contrary to the destiny and welfare of man" ("Kossuth's First Speech in Faneuil Hall, Thursday Evening, April 29, 1852," in *Old South Leaflets,* vol. 5, no. 111 [Boston: The Directors of the Old South Work, 1902], 225–44).

12. Hanckel, "South Carolina," xxi.

13. Benjamin H. Rutledge, *Memorial Day, May 10th, 1875* (N.p., n.d.), 4.

14. *Confederate Military History Extended Version,* 722.

15. Edward McCrady, Jr. to Edward McCrady L'Engle, 11 Oct. 1876, Edward McCrady L'Engle Papers. For a discussion of the role played by the rifle clubs in Hampton's election, see Holt, *Black Over White,* 203–4.

16. Reprinted in the *Charleston News and Courier,* 11 May 1899.

17. Walter Edgar adds Confederate monument building to this renewed conservative campaign. Edgar calls the Confederate monument erected on the statehouse grounds in 1879 a monument "to the old order, not the Confederacy." William Henry Trescot's words engraved on the monument honor "Men Whom Power Could Not Corrupt, Whom Death Could Not Terrify, Whom Defeat Could Not Dishonour." See Edgar, *South Carolina,* 424.

18. Richard Zuczek's *State of Rebellion: Reconstruction in South Carolina* (Columbia: University of South Carolina Press, 1996) makes a strong case for viewing white South Carolina's experience during Reconstruction as an act of war. In the immediate postwar years, Zuczek writes, "violence grew more coherent, political, and widespread, and so did conservative politics and political opposition" (5). Zuczek, however, uses "white South Carolinian" and "conservative" interchangeably, which this study does not do.

19. McCrady, *Registration of Electors,* 12.

20. E. Culpepper Clark, *Francis Warrington Dawson and the Politics of Reconstruction, 1874–1889* (University: University of Alabama Press, 1980), 71.

21. A South Carolinian [Belton O'Neall Townsend], "South Carolina Society," *Atlantic Monthly* (1877): 673–74.

22. Theodore G. Barker, *Address of Theo. G. Barker before the Washington Artillery Club on Their Anniversary, 22 February, 1876, at Hibernian Hall, Charleston, S.C.* (Charleston, S.C.: Lucas and Richardson, 1876), 5.

23. *Charleston Daily Courier,* 19 Nov. 1860.

24. Barker, *Address,* 7.

25. Rivers, *Address,* 18.

26. John Julius Pringle Smith, *Address Delivered before the South Carolina Historical Society on Their Twenty-Second Anniversary, May 25, 1877, by J. J. Pringle Smith, Esq., a Member* (Charleston, S.C.: Lucas and Richardson, 1879), 34.

27. McCrady, *Registration of Electors,* 3.

28. Ibid., 4, 5.

29. McCrady, *Review of the Resolutions,* 14.

30. A good account of the various legislative efforts to reconfigure the South Carolina polity is George Brown Tindall's "The Campaign for the Disfranchisement of Negroes in South Carolina," *Journal of Southern History* 15 (1949): 212–34. See also J. Morgan Kousser, *The Shaping of Southern Politics: Suffrage Restriction and the Establishment of the One-Party System, 1880–1910* (New Haven and London: Yale University Press, 1974), 84–91.

31. *Charleston News and Courier,* 6 Dec. 1881.

32. Ibid., 9 Dec. 1881. "Mahoneism" is a reference to the briefly successful, antielite, biracial political movement of Gen. William Mahone in Virginia in the mid-1870s. Conservative Charlestonians were not quick to forgive Mahone for his postwar political efforts. In 1885 the *Charleston News and Courier* ran Mahone's obituary under the title "Would He Had Died in Battle."

33. McCrady, *Registration of Electors,* 11.

34. William Porcher Miles, *Universal Education. How to Purify the Ballot-Box. Address before the Winyaw Indigo Society, on Their 28th Anniversary, at Georgetown, S.C., May 15th, 1882. By Hon. Wm. Porcher Miles, L.L.D., President of the South Carolina College* (Charleston, S.C.: The News and Courier Book Presses, 1882), 1, 6; H. R. Ravenel to McCrady, 18 Sept. 1889, Edward McCrady, Jr. Papers. A few conservative African American political leaders in South Carolina supported the literacy requirements McCrady suggested through the Eight-Box Law. William Holloway proclaimed, "Let those who need education to meet the requirements of the law, seek for it, and if they fail to secure enough for the needs of the hour, it will be their fault, and not the State's" (quoted in Tindall, *South Carolina Negroes,* 70). Holloway was, however, in a clear minority. Richard H. Cain expressed the more popular sentiment and logic that the African American voter "may not understand a great deal of the knowledge that is derived from books; he may not be generally familiar with the ways of the world, but he can, nevertheless, judge right from wrong" (quoted in Williamson, *After Slavery,* 337).

35. Thomas M. Hanckel, *Alumni Association. Address Delivered in the Hall of the House of Representatives before the Alumni of the University of South Carolina by Thomas M. Hanckel, One of the Alumni, December 6th, 1882* (Charleston, S.C.: The News and Courier Book Presses, 1882), 9–10.

36. Edward McCrady Jr., *The Necessity of Education as the Basis of Our Political System. An Address Delivered before the Euphemian Society of Erskine College, Due West, S.C., by Edward McCrady, Jr., of Charleston, S.C., June 28, 1880* (Charleston, S.C.: Walker, Evans, & Cogswell, 1880), 3.

37. Porcher, *Oration Delivered before the Inhabitants of Pineville,* 15.

38. McCrady, *Necessity of Education,* 13–14. For the Macaulay quote see Thomas Babington Macaulay, *Miscellanies,* vol. 1 (Boston and New York: Houghton Mifflin and Co., 1900), 272.

39. Ibid., 15.

40. Quoted in Lacy K. Ford, "Rednecks and Merchants: Economic Developments and Social Tensions in the South Carolina Upcountry, 1865–1900," *Journal of American History* 71 (1984): 309.

41. "A Southern Rebuke of Bourbonism," *The Nation* 27 (1878): 140.

42. Quoted in August Meier, *Negro Thought in America, 1880–1915: Racial Ideologies in the Age of Booker T. Washington* (Ann Arbor: University of Michigan Press, 1963), 70.

43. Tindall, *South Carolina Negroes,* 114–16.

44. Francis B. Simkins, *Pitchfork Ben Tillman: South Carolinian* (Baton Rouge: Louisiana State University Press, 1944); Cooper, *Conservative Regime;* Stephen Kantrowitz,

Ben Tillman and the Reconstruction of White Supremacy (Chapel Hill and London: University of North Carolina Press, 2000).

45. Dewey Grantham in *Southern Progressivism: The Reconciliation of Progress and Tradition* (Knoxville: University of Tennessee Press, 1983), summarized that the Tillman movement "offered no radical solutions, avoided third-party politics, and busied itself with capturing control of the Democratic party" (56).

46. *Charleston News and Courier,* 23 Jan. 1890.

47. Ibid.

48. Ibid.

49. Ibid.

50. Edward McCrady Jr., *Address Delivered to the South Carolina Military Academy, at the Annual Commencement, German Military Hall, Charleston, S.C., July 27th, 1887. By Gen'l Edward McCrady* (Charleston, S.C.: Walker, Evans, & Cogswell Co., 1887), 4.

51. Ibid., 6–7, 10.

52. Ibid., 5–6. McCrady thus put forward the conservative view of education—state-supported education for a select few to the ultimate good of all—to counter the more specific demands of the Tillman movement for the creation of a separate agricultural school to educate farmers toward better farming skills and knowledge. This issue was resolved shortly thereafter when Thomas Clemson passed away and left in his will provisions of land and money for the expressed purpose of starting an agricultural school.

53. The letter also appeared in the *Charleston News and Courier,* 17 Apr. 1888.

54. J. Middleton to Edward McCrady, Jr., 30 Apr. 1888; Robert Aldrich to Edward McCrady, Jr., 27 Apr. 1888; Julius Heyward to Edward McCrady, Jr., 29 Apr. 1888; John D. Edwards to Edward McCrady, Jr., 28 Apr. 1888—all in Edward McCrady, Jr. Papers.

55. Edward McCrady Jr., "Heroes of the Old Camden District, South Carolina, 1776–1861. An Address to the Survivors of Fairfield County, Delivered at Winnsboro, S.C., September 1, 1888. By Col. Edward McCrady, Jr.," *Southern Historical Society Papers* 16 (Jan.–Dec. 1888): 33–34.

56. Quoted in Simkins, *Pitchfork Ben Tillman,* 159.

57. "Our Danger and Our Duty," *Charleston News and Courier,* 18 Apr. 1890.

58. Quoted in Simkins, *Pitchfork Ben Tillman,* 159.

59. G. W. Gage to Edward McCrady, Jr., 18 Apr. 1890, Edward McCrady, Jr. Papers.

60. J. M. B. Reeves to Edward McCrady, Jr., 4 Dec. 1889, Edward McCrady, Jr. Papers.

61. M. C. Butler to Edward McCrady, Jr., 23 July 1890, Edward McCrady, Jr. Papers.

62. Ibid., 19 Aug. 1890, Edward McCrady, Jr. Papers.

63. Cooper, *Conservative Regime,* 185.

64. Simkins, *Pitchfork Ben Tillman,* 159.

65. Edward McCrady Jr., *Colonial Development. From an Emigrant Camp to a Well-Ordered State* (Charleston, S.C.: Lucas and Richardson, 1897), 2–4 (from Edward McCrady, Jr. Papers).

66. Kousser, *Shaping of Southern Politics,* 151.

67. Quoted in Mary J. Miller, *Suffrage Speeches by Negroes in the Constitutional Convention,* South Caroliniana Library, University of South Carolina, Columbia.

68. Tindall, *South Carolina Negroes,* 68–91.

69. Edward McCrady Jr. to Louisa Rebecca Barnwell, 9 Oct. 1899, Edward McCrady, Jr. Papers.

70. William Henry Trescot to Edward McCrady, Jr., 7 Sept. 1897, Edward McCrady, Jr. Papers. To demonstrate further the lack of scholarship in postwar southern conservatism, the literature on Trescot, an important antebellum figure, consists of dissertations, theses, and articles, few, if any, of which move chronologically beyond the war. Trescot lived until 1898. His case is not an isolated oversight.

71. Cooper, *Conservative Regime,* 207.

72. McCrady, "Heroes of the Old Camden District," 33–34.

73. Rivers, *Address,* 24.

74. Simkins, *Pitchfork Ben Tillman,* especially 455–69; Kantrowitz, *Ben Tillman.*

Chapter 4

1. Woodrow Wilson, "An Address on Robert E. Lee at the University of North Carolina [January 19, 1909]," in *The Papers of Woodrow Wilson,* edited by Arthur Link (Princeton, N.J.: Princeton University Press, 1974), 18:639.

2. Grantham, *Southern Progressivism.* Among historians of progressivism who have sounded similar themes is Henry May, who found "in the most dominant varieties of progressivism . . . some elements of actual conservatism or even, in the sense of return to the past, reaction" (Henry F. May, *The End of American Innocence: A Study of the First Years of Our Own Time, 1912–1917* [New York: Columbia University Press, Morningside edition, 1992], 26). See also Jack Temple Kirby, *Darkness at the Dawning: Race and Reform in the Progressive South* (Philadelphia, Pa.:

Lippincott, 1972); and William A. Link, *The Paradox of Southern Progressivism, 1880–1930* (Chapel Hill: University of North Carolina Press, 1992).

3. John A. Rice, *I Came Out of the Eighteenth Century* (New York and London: Harper and Brothers, 1942), 91–92.

4. *Echoes from "Hampton Day," May 14th, 1895. Compiled and Arranged for the Camp* (Charleston, S.C.: Walker, Evans, and Cogswell, 1895), 32–44.

5. Mayer, *Persistence of the Old Regime,* 136–37.

6. *Charleston News and Courier,* 28 Apr. 1898.

7. Ibid., 29 Apr. 1898.

8. Mayer, *Persistence of the Old Regime,* 136–37.

9. Edgar, *South Carolina,* 465.

10. *Charleston News and Courier,* 12 Nov. 1896.

11. Quoted in Ulrich B. Phillips's review of Jervey's *Robert Y. Hayne and His Times* in *American Historical Review* 15 (1910): 628.

12. Theodore D. Jervey Jr., "Conquered Germany," draft of an unpublished essay, Theodore D. Jervey Papers, folder 27, "ca. 1919–1930," South Carolina Historical Society, Charleston.

13. Theodore D. Jervey Jr., draft of untitled essay against the rise of the Ku Klux Klan, ca. 1920, Theodore D. Jervey Papers, folder 12.

14. Don Doyle, *New Men, New Cities, New South: Atlanta, Nashville, Charleston, Mobile, 1860–1910* (Chapel Hill and London: University of North Carolina Press, 1989), 159–88.

15. The editorials in *The Charleston World* were unsigned. Jervey's obituaries in the *Charleston News and Courier* (25 Jan. 1947, p. 2) and the *South Carolina Historical and Genealogical Magazine* (Jan. 1948, pp. 66–67) describe him as "an editorial writer" for *The Charleston World.* The Charleston city directories for 1889, 1890, and 1891 also list him as "editorial staff World-Budget Co."

16. "An Attack on Mr. Jervey," *The Charleston World,* 24 Aug. 1888, 8.

17. "The Public Is No Fool," *The Charleston World,* 18 Aug. 1888, 4.

18. Edward McCrady Jr., *Address Delivered to the South Carolina Military Academy, at the Annual Commencement, German Military Hall, Charleston, S.C., July 27th, 1887. By Gen'l Edward McCrady* (Charleston, S.C.: Walker, Evans, & Cogswell Co., 1887), 4.

19. *The Charleston World,* 11 Aug. 1888, 1.

20. Henry May writes of the progressive intellectuals, "When they said, as they constantly did, that power must be given back to the people, the word *people* did not mean everybody. . . . It meant the sound people under the right leadership" (May, *End of American Innocence,* 26).

21. *The Charleston World,* 11 Aug. 1888, 1.

22. Ibid., 23 Aug. 1888, 4. See also Cooper, *Conservative Regime,* 206.

23. Ibid., 10 Sept. 1888, 4.

24. "Ben Tillman. The Movement, the Man, and His Methods," *The Charleston World,* 24 June 1890, 1; Hampton M. Jarrell, *Wade Hampton and the Negro: The Road Not Taken* (Columbia: University of South Carolina Press, 1949), 52. Aldrich during this same time period wrote McCrady a letter of support during the libel suit against the latter.

25. "Letters from the People," *The Charleston World,* 20 June 1890, 2.

26. "Tillman as a Weathercock," *The Charleston World,* 12 Sept. 1891, 4. Further evidence suggesting that Jervey was the editorial writer for the paper comes indirectly from this piece. The paper broke form and noted for its readers that this particular article was not written by Jervey but by the managing editor of *The Charleston World,* Octavus Cohen.

27. Theodore D. Jervey Jr. to Yates Snowden, 1 Dec. 1912, Theodore D. Jervey, Jr. Papers; also quoted in John David Smith, *Black Judas: William Hannibal Thomas and the American Negro* (Athens and London: University of Georgia Press, 2000), 239.

28. David L. Carlton, *Mill and Town in South Carolina, 1880–1920* (Baton Rouge and London: Louisiana State University Press, 1982), 171–214; Edgar, *South Carolina,* 453–82; Robert Milton Burts, *Richard Irvine Manning and the Progressive Movement in South Carolina* (Columbia: University of South Carolina Press, 1974).

29. Daniel J. Singal, *The War Within: From Victorian to Modernist Thought in the South, 1919–1945* (Chapel Hill: University of North Carolina Press, 1982), 36.

30. Theodore D. Jervey Jr., drafts of essays, Theodore D. Jervey, Jr. Papers.

31. Idus A. Newby, *Black Carolinians: A History of Blacks in South Carolina from 1895 to 1968* (Columbia: University of South Carolina Press, 1973), 53–54.

32. John David Smith recently examined the correspondence between Jervey and Thomas in *Black Judas,* 238–44.

33. Theodore D. Jervey Jr., *The Elder Brother* (New York and Washington, D.C.: Neale Publishing Co., 1905), 3.

34. *New York Times,* 12 Aug. 1905, Saturday Supplement, 528.

35. It is not clear why Jervey chose this name for his fictionalized Charleston. Ellenton was the real-life sight of a bloody clash between black and white South Carolinians in 1876, but that Ellenton is located inland, near Hamburg and Augusta, Georgia. Jervey's Ellenton is a lowcountry city with a postwar "burnt district," similar to postwar Charleston.

36. Jervey, *Elder Brother,* 22. With this characterization, Jervey accepted the emerging interpretation of the war from the new generation of professional southern

scholars—John Spencer Bassett, Woodrow Wilson, and William P. Trent—contemporaries of Jervey who also mirrored his attempt to balance southern pride with national reunification. Thomas J. Pressly, in *Americans Interpret Their Civil War* (New York: The Free Press, 1965), discusses this generation's view of the conflict as "a war whose results were more important than its causes, a war whose prime significance lay in the fact that it had prepared the way for a new and better South by removing slavery and the type of sectionalism represented by secession" (187).

37. Jervey, *Elder Brother,* 178, 184. A number of scholars have noted the escalation of negative rhetoric regarding African American morality, intelligence, and physiology in late 1800s and early 1900s; see George Fredrickson, *The Black Image in the White Mind: The Debate on Afro-American Character and Destiny, 1817–1914* (New York: Harper and Row, 1971), 228–82; Thomas Gossett, *Race: The History of an Idea in America* (New York: Schocken Books, 1965), 253–309; and Idus A. Newby, *Anti-Negro Thought in America, 1900–1930* (Baton Rouge: Louisiana State University Press, 1965), 19–81.

38. Jervey, *Elder Brother,* 80, 84, 139. The Samuel Jenkinson character is certainly a re-creation of a postwar African American politician and lawyer in Charleston, Samuel J. Dickerson. In his last book, *The Slave Trade,* Jervey describes Dickerson "as a slave a bricklayer, but as a local freeman, dropping his tools for a higher pursuit and destined to become the mountebank of the bar" (Theodore D. Jervey Jr., *The Slave Trade: Slavery and Color* [Columbia, S.C.: The State Co., 1925], 126).

39. Jervey, *Elder Brother,* 138, 205, 207. Jervey occasionally raised insightful questions about the very solutions he proposed. In the latter scene Jervey describes Washington's thoughts as he considered Rupert's advice: "Washington knew he could love Rupert, no matter what side Rupert was on; but would Rupert continue to love him if he was in opposition to the white people seemingly?" (206).

40. Ibid., 352, 386, 387, 390. Jervey demonstrated the popular notion among white southerners that the blacks would descend or even disappear with freedom (see Fredrickson, *Black Image in the White Mind,* 228–82).

41. Jervey, *Elder Brother,* 69, 119, 191, 413.

42. Theodore D. Jervey Jr., "Love Blinds?," unpub. ms., Theodore D. Jervey Jr. Papers, 15.

43. Ibid., 28.

44. Ibid., 28–29.

45. David D. Wallace, "The Democratization of an Old Commonwealth," D. D. Wallace Papers, South Carolina Historical Society, Charleston, 14.

46. Jervey, "Love Blinds?," 33, 40.

47. Ibid., 236–37.

48. In a March 1926 letter Jervey revealed that he had worked on *The Slave Trade* for sixteen years before finally seeing it published (Theodore J. Jervey to Francis W. Dawson II, 8 Mar. 1926, Francis Warrington Dawson I and II Papers, Special Collections, Perkins Library, Duke University, Durham, North Carolina).

49. The link to the Old South is evident before the reader leaves the title page. On the opposite page is a picture of Wade Hampton. Another contemporary observer of the "race problem," Alfred Holt Stone, also took pains to tie his views to those of an older generation. The dedication to Stone's *Studies in the American Race Problem* (New York: Doubleday, 1908) reads: "To my father and mother as connecting links to the old regime."

50. Jervey, *Slave Trade,* 4, 48–54, 59, 20. The upas is a large tree that produces a poisonous berry.

51. Ibid., 170–71.

52. Ibid., 239–40.

53. Ibid., 254, 185–86. Jervey was likely referring to *Our Brother in Black: His Freedom and His Future* (New York: Phillips and Hunt, 1881) by Atticus Haygood. Haygood was a late-nineteenth-century white southerner who spoke passionately and compassionately of the common humanity of both races.

54. Ibid.

55. Paul Rohrbach, *German World Policies,* translated by Edmund von Mach (New York: Macmillan, 1915), 135.

56. Theodore D. Jervey to Francis W. Dawson II, 8 Mar. 1926, Francis Warrington Dawson I and II Papers.

57. See J. G. La Guerre, *Enemies of Empire* (St. Augustine, Trinidad: The College Press, 1984), 65.

58. Jervey, *Slave Trade,* 186, 182.

59. Ibid., 202, 282.

60. Ibid., 279–80.

61. Newby, *Black Carolinians,* 194.

62. Benjamin R. Tillman to Theodore R. Jervey, 16 Mar. 1914, Theodore D. Jervey Jr. Papers. Tillman still liked and respected Jervey. He added in a later letter, "I have always believed you to be honest and clean and above suspicion in your dealings with men and affairs, and nothing you may say to me, or do, is likely to change that opinion. . . . In fact, you are the one prominent man in Charleston upon whom I can rely implicitly in everything" (Tillman to Jervey, 24 Mar. 1914, Theodore D. Jervey Jr. Papers).

Chapter 5

1. William Watts Ball Diary, vol. 1, 25 Apr. 1916, 11, William Watts Ball Papers.

2. Ball, *The State That Forgot: South Carolina's Surrender to Democracy* (Indianapolis, Ind.: Bobbs-Merrill Company, 1932), 14. See also John D. Stark, *Damned Upcountryman: William Watts Ball, A Study in American Conservatism* (Durham, N.C.: Duke University Press, 1968). Even though Stark's biography was extremely useful for this chapter, Ball did not make a convincing "upcountryman" even by his own admission. In the mid-1930s Ball wrote to Dr. Edward McCrady, Edward McCrady Jr.'s nephew, that he had "long ago been 'domesticated'"; the Charlestonians, he explained, "took me in, and I would be at home now nowhere else" (William Watts Ball to Dr. Edward McCrady, 11 Mar. 1922, William Watts Ball Papers). Ball typed the wrong year at the top of the letter; there are references to events occurring in 1936 in the text.

3. Mary Katherine Davis Cann, "The Morning After: South Carolina in the Jazz Age" (Ph.D. diss., University of South Carolina, 1984), 9–12, 337–400, 353; Edgar, *South Carolina,* 485–95.

4. Ball, "Primogeniture" [3 June 1887], copy of speech in William Watts Ball Papers.

5. Carlton, *Mill and Town in South Carolina,* chaps. 3, 4; *Charleston News and Courier,* 16 Dec. 1887.

6. For discussion of the Blease administration see David Duncan Wallace, *South Carolina: A Short History, 1520–1948* (Chapel Hill: University of North Carolina Press, 1951), 657–64; Carlton, *Mill and Town in South Carolina,* 215–72; and Bryant Simon, *A Fabric of Defeat: The Politics of South Carolina Millhands, 1910–1948* (Chapel Hill and London: University of North Carolina Press, 1998), 11–58.

7. Joseph W. Barnwell to William Watts Ball, 30 Dec. 1912, William Watts Ball Papers.

8. David Carlton calls the years between Blease's election in 1910 and the entry of the United States into World War I "a period of upheaval impressive even by the tumultuous standards set by the state's postbellum history" (Carlton, *Mill and Town in South Carolina,* 215).

9. Ball, "The Industrial Revolution in South Carolina" (1911), reprinted in Ball, *The Editor and the Republic: Papers and Addresses of William Watts Ball,* edited by Anthony Harrigan (Chapel Hill: University of North Carolina Press, 1954), 9–10.

10. Ibid., 11.

11. Ball to J. C. Hemphill, 28 May 1912, William Watts Ball Papers.

12. Ball, "Industrial Revolution in South Carolina," 11.

13. Ball to J. C. Hemphill, 8 Sept. 1914, William Watts Ball Papers.

14. Ball, "Back to Calhoun" (1917), reprinted in Ball, *Editor and the Republic,* 38–39.

15. Ball, "Are the Negroes Free?" (1914), reprinted in Ball, *Editor and the Republic,* 29–34.

16. Ibid.

17. Ball to Frederick Calvin Norton, 11 Mar. 1916, William Watts Ball Papers.

18. Carlton, *Mill and Town in South Carolina,* 158–59.

19. Ball, "Are the Negroes Free?," 32–34.

20. Ibid.

21. "Are the Negroes Free?" also gives the reader some of Ball's sloppier analysis. Sketching out a historical outline of freedom versus slavery in the 1800s, Ball wrote, "I hold that, apart from the question of human slavery, [William Lloyd] Garrison and his gang of Abolitionists needlessly forced a war and prevented peaceful emancipation." Garrison, it is safe to say, would have agreed wholeheartedly that "apart from the question of human slavery," the war was indeed needless.

22. George B. Tindall, *The Emergence of the New South, 1913–1945* (Baton Rouge: Louisiana State University Press, 1967), 160; Michael O'Brien, *The Idea of the American South, 1920–1941* (Baltimore, Md. and London: Johns Hopkins University Press, 1979), 16; Newby, *Black Carolinians,* 185–86.

23. Ball, "Back to Aristocracy" (1918), reprinted in Ball, *Editor and the Republic,* 62.

24. William Watts Ball Diary, 13 Jan. 1918, 119, William Watts Ball Papers.

25. Edgar, *South Carolina,* 481.

26. Ball to Oswald Garrison Villard, 15 June 1932, William Watts Ball Papers.

27. W. W. Johnson to Ball, 9 Jan. 1918, William Watts Ball Papers.

28. William Watts Ball Diary, 14 Aug. 1918, 130, William Watts Ball Papers.

29. Ball to Frederick Calvin Norton, 8 Mar. 1919, William Watts Balls Papers.

30. William Watts Ball Diary, vol. 4, 9 Nov. 1918, 236, William Watts Ball Papers. Ball's views of the "Big Business" class at this time were captured vividly in his diary. In 1916 he recorded a conversation regarding a possible American invasion of Mexico he had with a Mr. Baldwin, a northern owner of southern textile mills, whom Ball described as "a well-to-do, well-fed, well groomed business man." Ball recalled Baldwin as saying, "Why Mr. Ball, those states of Sonora and Chihuahua are the finest grazing grounds in the world—and we need grazing grounds!" Ball wrote later, "That was a typical expression of the

bold, enterprising, gross, rapacious, capitalistic class." See William Watts Ball Diary, vol. 2, 1 July 1916, 1, William Watts Ball Papers.

31. Ibid., 11 Nov. 1918, 238.

32 T. R. Waring to Ball, 10 Oct. 1919, William Watts Ball Papers.

33. James F. Byrnes to Ball, 18 Jan. 1920, William Watts Ball Papers.

34. Barbara Woods Aba-Mecha, "Black Woman Activist in Twentieth Century South Carolina: Modjeska Monteith Simkins" (Ph.D. diss., Emory University, 1978), 154–57.

35. Cann, "Morning After," 9–10.

36. Edgar, *South Carolina,* 485.

37. William Watts Ball Diary, vol. 5, 18 Oct. 1920, 127, William Watts Ball Papers. Ball's criticism of the Republicans at this time was that they would return to the days of "Hannaism," as he called it—an extreme position of laissez-faire and economic concentration. Warren G. Harding was, in Ball's words, the "amiable ass" that big business had put up to please the public and win votes without divulging their objectives as a ruling party.

38. Ibid., 21 Oct. 1920, 128–29.

39. Letter from John A. Law to Ball quoted in Tindall, *Emergence of the New South,* 333.

40. William Watts Ball Diary, 23 Dec. 1923, 156, William Watts Ball Papers. Sinha in *Counterrevolution of Slavery* shows how conservatives' linked abolitionism with socialism in the 1850s (see her chap. 8).

41. Unpublished manuscript on socialism ["1912" written on top of front page] in WWBP, Special Collections Library, Duke University, Durham, N.C.

42. Ball to J. F. J. Caldwell, 6 Jan. 1919, William Watts Ball Papers.

43. Ball to John P. Grace, 3 July 1934, William Watts Ball Papers.

44. William Watts Ball Diary, vol. 6, Dec. 1923, 156, William Watts Ball Papers.

45. Ball to John P. Grace, 3 July 1934, William Watts Ball Papers.

46. William Watts Ball Diary, vol. 5, 26 Aug. 1920, 110; 24 July 1920, 19, William Watts Ball Papers.

47. Ibid., vol. 7, 28 Oct. 1928, 214.

48. Ball to C. J. Thackston, 15 Oct. 1929, William Watts Ball Papers.

49. Edwin Hoffman, "The Genesis of the Modern Movement for Civil Rights in South Carolina," in *The Negro in Depression and War: Prelude to Revolution, 1930–1945,* edited by Bernard Sternsher (Chicago, Ill.: Quadrangle Books, 1969), 203–4.

50. William Watts Ball Diary, 7 Sept. 1931, William Watts Ball Papers.

51. Ibid., 25 May 1930.

52. Hoffman, "Genesis of the Modern Movement," 200.

53. Aba-Mecha, "Black Woman Activist," 161.

54. William Watts Ball Diary, vol. 7, 25 May 1930, William Watts Ball Papers. Ball's views during these years mirrored Donald Davidson's. Despite his claim that the "Negro question" was low on his list of priorities, Davidson in 1929 wrote that his thoughts on the subject were of "the *better* Southern view, not the view of the riff-raff. This means segregation, no social equality, probably economic subjugation for a long time to come; it does not mean that the Negro should suffer political injustice, as in the courts, or be the object of any vindictive oppression. I am firmly with the Southern states that keep the vote out of the Negro's hands as far as possible, but that is no real injustice. . . . I see no objection to a *qualified* Negro suffrage" (quoted in O'Brien, *Idea of the American South,* 17).

55. Ibid., vol. 7, 25 May 1930, 352.

56. Ball to Frederick Calvin Norton, 11 Mar. 1916, William Watts Ball Papers.

57. William Watts Ball Diary, vol. 11, 12 June 1938, 11, William Watts Ball Papers.

58. Ralph Ellison, *Invisible Man* (New York: Random House, 1952), 3.

59. Ball, *State That Forgot.*

60. Cann, "Morning After," 2–3.

61. Michael O'Brien noted the function of the "myth" or the idea of the South during these same years. "The function of the myth was complicated," he wrote, suggesting that "precisely its value lay in its organic counterpoint to a confusing and accelerating society." The soothing abilities of the myth were but one function. O'Brien also found Allen Tate's observation that as a southern conservative "our entire program is based on the assumed fact that the tradition is there to work on; otherwise we are only American liberals offering a new panacea and pretending to a concrete background that doesn't exist." See O'Brien, *Idea of the American South,* 223, 149.

62. Ball's book fits somewhere in between Ben Robertson's *Red Hills and Cotton* and William Percy's *Lanterns on the Levee.* Not nearly as well written as either or them, Ball's work manages to mix some of Percy's elitism with Robertson's earthiness.

63. Ball, *State That Forgot,* 110–11.

64. Ibid., 111.

65. Ibid., 113.

66. Ibid., 121.

67. Ibid., 121. Hearkening back to an earlier theme in his essay "Are the Negroes Free?," Ball in the same chapter records his mother's slavery-era memory of "Aunt Mary." He describes "Aunt Mary" as one who "was born a slave in 1838,

and on December 11, 1917, two weeks before she was seventy-nine, died a slave" (117). He then goes on to describe through his mother's memory "Aunt Mary's" life of joy and comfort provided by the Ball family.

68. Ibid., 200–201.

69. Edgar, *South Carolina,* 499.

70. Ball to Clement Ripley, 14 Sept. 1934, William Watts Ball Papers; see also Simon, *Fabric of Defeat,* 79–187.

71. William Watts Ball Diary, 31 Dec. 1932, William Watts Ball Papers. George B. Tindall has noted that South Carolina was already receiving federal relief assistance of nearly four million dollars from President Hoover's Reconstruction Finance Corporation. Late in his term Hoover reluctantly permitted the Reconstruction Finance Corporation to be used in more direct relief efforts as opposed to his earlier intention of solidifying the top of the nation's economic structure only. See Tindall, *Emergence of the New South,* 374.

72. Ibid., vol. 9, 14 May 1933, 58, 59–60. W. E. B. Du Bois made a similar observation in 1941. He wrote that with the New Deal "there came unemployment and relief . . . [and] a direct connection between politics and industry, between government and work, between voting and wages, such as the South was born believing was absolutely impossible and fundamentally wrong" (quoted in Patricia Sullivan, *Days of Hope: Race and Democracy in the New Deal Era* [Chapel Hill and London: University of North Carolina Press, 1996], 69).

73. Ibid., vol. 9, 17 June 1935, 255.

74. Ball to George L. Buist, 3 Nov. 1934, William Watts Ball Papers.

75. Ball's best friend, Fitzhugh McMaster, in 1938 wrote and scolded him, "You do nothing but write about Roosevelt"; McMaster urged him to take on other matters as well, "You will have to diversify" (Fitzhugh McMaster to William Watts Ball, 3 Feb. 1938, William Watts Ball Papers; also quoted in Stark, *Damned Upcountryman* [179], a solid, and the only, account of Ball's life).

76. William Watts Ball Diary, vol. 10, 16 Sept. 1935, 1, WWBP.

77. Ibid.

78. Ibid., 6 Sept. 1936, 93.

79. For an account, see Wallace, *South Carolina,* 605. Wallace's interpretation of this period recounts the end of Reconstruction with a view almost identical to Edward McCrady's assessment as it was happening.

80. William Watts Ball Diary, 6 Sept. 1936, 93, William Watts Ball Papers. On the movement of black voters into the Democratic Party, see Nancy Weiss, *Farewell to the Party of Lincoln: Black Politics in the Age of FDR* (Princeton, N.J.: Princeton University Press, 1983); and Harvard Sitkoff, *A New Deal for Blacks: The Emergence*

of Civil Rights as a National Issue (New York and Oxford: Oxford University Press, 1978).

81. Ibid., 13 Sept. 1936, 95.

82. Ibid., 24 July 1936, 71.

83. Ibid., vol.10, 19 Dec. 1936, 131.

84. Ibid.

85. See Simon, *Fabric of Defeat,* 90–108

86. Ball to Sara [Ball Copeland?], 24 Apr. 1938, William Watts Ball Papers.

87. William Watts Ball Diary, 13 July 1937, 200, William Watts Ball Papers.

88. Ball to Bernard M. Baruch, 11 Mar. 1938, Willian Watts Ball Papers.

89. Josiah W. Bailey to Ball, 24 Sept. 1937, William Watts Ball Papers.

90. Aba-Mecha, "Black Woman Activist," 167–77; Sullivan, *Days of Hope,* 143–45.

91. Ball to Fitzhugh McMaster, 6 June 1938, William Watts Ball Papers.

92. James Emery Brooks, "The Bolshevik Conspiracy" to Ball, 1 Nov. 1937, William Watts Ball Papers; Matt Walker to Ball, 23 May 1938, William Watts Ball Papers.

93. Josiah W. Bailey to Ball, 4 Dec. 1943, William Watts Ball Papers.

94. Ball, "A Statement of Belief," reprinted in Ball, *Editor and the Republic,* 208.

95. Sullivan, *Days of Hope,* 189–91.

96. Tinsley E. Yarbrough, *A Passion for Justice: J. Waties Waring and Civil Rights* (New York and Oxford: Oxford University Press, 1987), 69.

97. Ball, "States' Rights 1948 Issue," *New York Herald Tribune,* 22 Feb. 1948, sec. 2, p. 7.

98. Ball, "Thurmond for President," *Charleston News and Courier,* 5 Nov. 1948.

Epilogue

1. DuBose Heyward, "The Negro in the Low-Country," in *The Carolina Low-Country,* edited by Augustine T. Smythe et al. (New York: Macmillan, 1931), 184.

2. DuBose Heyward, *Mamba's Daughters* (Garden City, N.J.: Doubleday, Doran and Company, Inc., 1929), 46.

3. Fritz Stern, *The Politics of Cultural Despair: A Study in the Rise of the Germanic Ideology* (Berkeley, Los Angeles, and London: University of California Press, 1961), 152.

4. William Watts Ball Diary, 24 July 1936, 71, William Watts Ball Papers.

5. Simon, *Fabric for Defeat,* 96, 91.

6. *Charleston Daily Courier,* 19 Nov. 1860.

7. "Why a Democratic Senator Turned Republican," *U. S. News and World Report* (28 Sept. 1964): 83–84. Transcript of televised address by Strom Thurmond, originally broadcast on 16 Sept., 1964.

BIBLIOGRAPHY

Manuscript Collections

Ball, William Watts. Papers. Special Collections, Perkins Library, Duke University, Durham, North Carolina.

Butler, Matthew C. Papers. The South Caroliniana Library, University of South Carolina, Columbia.

Dawson, Francis Warrington I and II. Papers. Special Collections, Perkins Library, Duke University, Durham, North Carolina.

Grimball, John Berkeley. Diary. Southern Historical Collection, University of North Carolina, Chapel Hill.

Jervey, Theodore D., Jr. Papers. South Carolina Historical Society, Charleston.

L'Engle, Edward McCrady. Papers. Southern Historical Collection, University of North Carolina, Chapel Hill.

McCrady, Edward, Jr. Papers. South Carolina Historical Society, Charleston.

Picketts, John T. Papers. Alderman Library, University of Virginia, Charlottesville.

Porcher, Frederick A. Papers. Archives, Special Collections, Robert Scott Small Library, College of Charleston, Charleston, South Carolina.

————. Papers. South Carolina Historical Society, Charleston.

————. Papers. South Caroliniana Library, University of South Carolina, Columbia.

Wallace, David D. Papers. South Carolina Historical Society, Charleston.

Primary Source Books, Pamphlets, Speeches

Ball, William Watts. *The Editor and the Republic: Papers and Addresses of William Watts Ball.* Edited by Anthony Harrigan. Chapel Hill: University of North Carolina Press, 1954.

————. *The State That Forgot: South Carolina's Surrender to Democracy.* Indianapolis, Ind.: Bobbs-Merrill, 1932.

Barker, Theodore G. *Address of Theo. G. Barker before the Washington Artillery Club on Their Anniversary, 22 February, 1876, at Hibernian Hall, Charleston, S.C.* Charleston, S.C.: Lucas and Richardson, 1876.

Echoes from "Hampton Day," May 14th, 1895. Compiled and Arranged for the Camp. Charleston, S.C.: Walker, Evans, & Cogswell, 1895.

Hanckel, Thomas M. *Alumni Association. Address Delivered in the Hall of the House of Representatives before the Alumni of the University of South Carolina by Thomas M. Hanckel,*

One of the Alumni, December 6th, 1882. Charleston, S.C.: The News and Courier Book Presses, 1882.

———. *Sermons by the Right Reverend Stephen Elliott, D.D., Late Bishop of Georgia. With a Memoir, by Thomas M. Hanckel, Esq.* New York: Pott and Amery, 1867.

———. "South Carolina—Her State Sovereignty." *De Bow's Review* 29 (20 September 1860).

Jervey, Theodore. *The Elder Brother.* New York and Washington, D.C.: Neale Publishing Co., 1905.

———. "Love Blinds," unpublished manuscript, Theodore D. Jervey, Jr. Papers, South Carolina Historical Society, Charleston.

———. "A Sign of the Times." *Harper's Weekly* 35 (January 1891): 82–83.

———. *The Slave Trade: Slavery and Color.* Columbia, S.C.: The State Co., 1925.

McCrady, Edward, Jr. *Address Delivered to the South Carolina Military Academy, at the Annual Commencement, German Military Hall, Charleston, S.C., July 27th, 1887. By Gen'l Edward McCrady.* Charleston: Walker, Evans, & Cogswell, 1887.

———. *Articles on Political Parties, and Their Relation to Each Other.* Charleston, S.C.: News and Courier Book and Job Presses, 1878.

———. "Before Company A (Gregg's Brigade), First S.C. Volunteers, at the Reunion at Williston, Barnwell County, S.C. 14th July, 1882." *Southern Historical Society Papers* 16 (1888): 246–61.

———. *Colonial Development. From an Emigrant Camp to a Well-Ordered State.* Charleston, S.C.: Lucas and Richardson, 1897.

———. "Heroes of the Old Camden District, South Carolina, 1776–1861. An Address to the Survivors of Fairfield County, Delivered at Winnsboro, S.C., September 1, 1888. By Col. Edward McCrady, Jr." *Southern Historical Society Papers* 16 (January–December 1888): 1–35.

———. *History of South Carolina in the Revolution, 1775–1780.* New York: Macmillan, 1901, 1902.

———. *The Necessity of Education as the Basis of Our Political System. An Address Delivered before the Euphemian Society of Erskine College, Due West, S.C., by Edward McCrady, Jr., of Charleston, S.C., June 28, 1880.* Charleston, S.C.: Walker, Evans, & Cogswell, 1880.

———. *Registration of Electors.* Special Collections, College of Charleston, Charleston, S.C.

———. *A Review of the Resolutions of the Press Conference.* Charleston, S.C.: Walker, Evans, & Cogswell, 1870.

Miles, William Porcher. *Universal Education. How to Purify the Ballot-Box. Address before the Winyaw Indigo Society on their 28th Anniversary, at Georgetown, S.C., May 15th,*

1882. By Hon. Wm. Porcher Miles, L.L.D., President of the South Carolina College. Charleston, S.C.: The News and Courier Book Presses, 1882.

Miller, Mary J. *Suffrage Speeches by Negroes in the Constitutional Convention.* South Caroliniana Library, University of South Carolina, Columbia.

Porcher, Frederick A. "Address Pronounced at the Inauguration of the South Carolina Historical Society, June 28, 1857, by F. A. Porcher." In *Collections of the South Carolina Historical Society.* Charleston, S.C.: S. G. Courtenay and Company, 1857.

———. "Bancroft's History of the United States." *Russell's Magazine* 3 (September 1858): 521–30.

———. "The Conflict of Capital and Labor." *Russell's Magazine* 3 (July 1858): 289–98.

———. *Eulogy on the Late Hon. John C. Calhoun, Delivered before the Cliosophic and Chrestomathic Societies of the College of Charleston, on Thursday, June 6th, 1850.* Charleston, S.C.: John Russell, 1850.

———. "False Views of History." *Southern Quarterly Review* n.s. 6 (July 1852): 23–48.

———. *Governor Rutledge. The Attacks of a Brooklyn Editor Vigorously Repelled. A Masterly Review of the Great South Carolinian's Character.* Wilson Library, Pamphlets Collection, University of North Carolina, Chapel Hill.

———. *History of the Santee Canal. Dedicated to the South Carolina Historical Society, 1875. By F. A. Porcher.* Charleston: South Carolina Historical Society, 1903.

———. "The Last Chapter in the History of Reconstruction in South Carolina." *Southern Historical Society Papers* 12 (1884): 173–81, 193–205, 241–53, 309–21, 554–58; 13 (1885): 47–87.

———. "Memoirs of Frederick Augustus Porcher." *South Carolina Historical Magazine* 45 (1944): 65–80, 135–47, 212–19; 46 (1945): 30–40, 80–89, 146–56, 200–216; 47 (1946): 25–39, 78–92, 140–58, 198–208; 48 (1947): 32–52, 83–108, 150–62, 214–27; 49 (1948): 20–25.

———. "The Nature and Claims of Paradox." *Russell's Magazine* 1 (September 1857): 481–89.

———. *An Oration Delivered before the Inhabitants of Pineville, So. Ca. on Monday, July 4th, 1831, the 56th Anniversary of the Declaration of Independence. By Frederick A. Porcher, Esq.* Edited by Samuel Gaillard Stoney. Charleston, S.C.: J. W. Burges, 1831.

———. "Southern and Northern Civilizations Contrasted." *Russell's Magazine* 1 (May 1857): 97–107.

———. "Webster's Dictionary." *Russell's Magazine* 5 (August 1859): 410–19.

Porter, W. D. *College and Collegians. An Address Delivered by W. D. Porter, before the Alumni Association of the College of Charleston, on Commencement Day, 28th March, 1871.* Charleston, S.C.: Walker, Evans, & Cogswell, Printers and Stationers, 1871.

Rivers, William J. *Address Delivered before the South Carolina Historical Society on Their Twenty-First Anniversary, May 19, 1876.* Charleston, S.C.: The News and Courier Job Presses, 1876.

Rutledge, Benjamin H. "Memorial Day, May 10th, 1875." Duke University, Perkins Library, Durham, N.C.

Smith, John Julius Pringle. *Address Delivered before the South Carolina Historical Society on Their Twenty-second Anniversary, May 25th, 1877, by J. J. Pringle Smith, Esq. a Member.* Charleston, S.C.: Lucas and Richardson, 1879.

A South Carolinian [Belton O'Neall Townsend]. "South Carolina Society." *Atlantic Monthly* (June 1877): 673–74.

"A Southern Rebuke of Bourbonism." *The Nation* 27 (5 September 1878): 140.

Newspapers and Government Documents

Charleston Daily Courier
Charleston News and Courier
The Charleston World
New York Herald Tribune
The New York Times
U.S. News and World Report
1860 Census. Charleston County, South Carolina. Slave Schedules, Charleston County Library, Charleston, South Carolina.

Secondary Works

Aba-Mecha, Barbara Woods. "Black Woman Activist in Twentieth Century South Carolina: Modjeska Monteith Simkins." Ph.D. diss., Emory University, 1978.

Anderson, Olive. "The Political Uses of History in Mid-Nineteenth Century England." *Past and Present* 36 (April 1967): 87–105.

Ayers, Edward. *Vengeance and Justice: Crime and Punishment in the Nineteenth-Century American South.* New York: Oxford University Press, 1984.

Baltzell, E. Digby. *The Protestant Establishment: Aristocracy and Caste in America.* New York: Random House, 1964.

Bishir, Catharine. "Landmarks of Power: Rebuilding a Southern Past." *Southern Cultures* (Inaugural Issue 1993): 5–45.

Blansard, Paul. "Communism in Southern Cotton Mills." *Nation* 128 (1929): 500–501.

Bradford, M. E. *Remembering Who We Are: Observations of a Southern Conservative.* Athens: University of Georgia Press, 1985.

Burke, Edmund. *Further Reflections on the Revolution in France.* Edited by Daniel E. Ritchie. Indianapolis, Ind.: Liberty Fund, Inc., 1992.

Burts, Robert Milton. *Richard Irvine Manning and the Progressive Movement in South Carolina.* Columbia: University of South Carolina Press, 1974.

Calhoun, Richard J. "Ante-Bellum Literary Thought: *Russell's Magazine.*" *Southern Literary Journal* (Fall 1970): 89–103.

Cann, Mary Katherine Davis. "The Morning After: South Carolina in the Jazz Age." Ph.D. diss., University of South Carolina, 1984.

Cannadine, David. *The Decline and Fall of the British Aristocracy.* New Haven, Conn.: Yale University Press, 1990.

Carlton, David. *Mill and Town in South Carolina, 1880–1920.* Baton Rouge and London: Louisiana State University Press, 1982.

Cash, W. J. *The Mind of the South.* New York: A. A. Knopf, 1941.

Cauthen, Charles E., ed. *Family Letters of the Three Wade Hamptons, 1782–1901.* Columbia: University of South Carolina Press, 1953.

Clark, E. Culpepper. *Francis Warrington Dawson and the Politics of Reconstruction, 1874–1889.* University: University of Alabama Press, 1980.

Confederate Military History Extended Version. Wilmington, N.C.: Broadfoot Publishing Company, 1987.

Cooper, William J., Jr. *The Conservative Regime: South Carolina, 1877–1890.* Baton Rouge: Louisiana State University Press, 1968.

Dew, Charles B. *Apostles of Disunion: Southern Secession Commissioners and the Causes of the Civil War.* Charlottesville and London: University of Virginia Press, 2001.

Doyle, Don H. *New Men, New Cities, New South: Atlanta, Nashville, Charleston, Mobile, 1860–1910.* Chapel Hill and London: University of North Carolina Press, 1989.

Eaton, Clement. *The Waning of the Old South Civilization, 1860–1880s.* Athens: University of Georgia Press, 1968.

Edgar, Walter B. *South Carolina: A History.* Columbia: University of South Carolina Press, 1998.

Egerton, John. *To Speak Now Against the Day: The Generation Before the Civil Rights Movement.* New York: Alfred A. Knopf, Inc., 1994.

Ellison, Ralph. *The Invisible Man.* New York: Vintage Books, 1972 edition.

Faust, Drew Gilpin. *James Henry Hammond and the Old South: A Design for Mastery.* Baton Rouge and London: Louisiana State University Press, 1982.

————. *A Sacred Circle: The Dilemma of the Intellectual in the Old South, 1840–1860.* Philadelphia: University of Pennsylvania Press, 1986.

————, ed. *The Ideology of Slavery: Proslavery Thought in the Antebellum South, 1830–1860.* Baton Rouge and London: Louisiana State University Press, 1981.

Fields, Barbara Jeanne. "Ideology and Race in American History." In *Region, Race, and Reconstruction: Essays in Honor of C. Vann Woodward,* edited by J. MorganKousser and James M. McPherson. New York and Oxford: Oxford University Press, 1982.

Fine, Sidney. *Laissez Faire and the General-Welfare State: A Study in Conflict in American Thought, 1865–1901.* Ann Arbor: University of Michigan Press, 1956.

Foner, Eric. *Free Soil, Free Labor, Free Men: The Ideology of the Republican Party before the Civil War.* Oxford, London, and New York: Oxford University Press, 1970.

————. *Nothing but Freedom: Emancipation and Its Legacy.* Baton Rouge and London: Louisiana State University Press, 1983.

Ford, Lacy. *Origins of Southern Radicalism, 1800–1860.* Oxford and New York: Oxford University Press, 1988.

————. "Rednecks and Merchants: Economic Developments and Social Tensions in the South Carolina Upcountry, 1865–1900." *Journal of American History* 71 (September 1984): 309.

————. "Republics and Democracy." In *The Meaning of South Carolina History: Essays in Honor of George C. Rogers, Jr.* Columbia: University of South Carolina Press, 1991.

Foster, Gaines. *Ghosts of the Confederacy: Defeat, the Lost Cause, and the Emergence of the New South, 1865 to 1913.* New York and Oxford: Oxford University Press, 1987.

Fox-Genovese, Elizabeth. "The Anxiety of History: The Southern Confrontation with Modernity." *Southern Cultures* (Inaugural Issue 1993): 65–82.

————. *Within the Plantation Household: Black and White Women of the Old South.* Chapel Hill and London: University of North Carolina Press, 1988.

Fredrickson, George. *The Black Image in the White Mind: The Debate on Afro-American Character and Destiny, 1817–1914.* New York: Harper and Row, 1971.

Freehling, William W. *Prelude to Civil War: The Nullification Controversy in South Carolina, 1816–1836.* New York: Harper and Row, 1966.

Furet, Francois. "Civilization and Barbarism in Gibbon's History." In *Edmund Gibbon and the Decline and Fall of the Roman Empire,* edited by G. W. Bowersock, John Clive, and Stephen R. Graubard. Cambridge and London: Harvard University Press, 1977.

Gallagher, Gary W., and Alan T. Nolan, eds. *The Myth of the Lost Cause and Civil War History.* Bloomington: University of Indiana Press, 2000.

Garson, Robert. *The Democratic Party and the Politics of Sectionalism, 1941–1948*. Baton Rouge and London: Louisiana State University Press, 1974.

Genovese, Eugene. *Roll, Jordan, Roll: The World the Slaves Made*. New York: Pantheon, 1975.

————. *The Slaveholders' Dilemma: Freedom and Progress in Southern Conservative Thought, 1820–1860*. Columbia: University of South Carolina Press, 1992.

————. *The Southern Tradition: The Achievement and Limitations of an American Conservatism*. Cambridge and London: Harvard University Press, 1994.

————. *The World the Slaveholders Made: Two Essays in Interpretation*. Middletown, Conn.: Wesleyan University Press, 1988 edition.

Gladstone, William E. "'Locksley Hall' and The Jubilee." *The Nineteenth Century* 113 (January 1887): 1–18.

Gooch, G. P. *History and Historians in the Nineteenth Century*. Boston, Mass.: Beacon Press, 1913.

Gossett, Thomas. *Race: The History of an Idea in America*. New York: Schocken Books, 1965.

Grantham, Dewey. *Southern Progressivism: The Reconciliation of Progress and Tradition*. Knoxville: University of Tennessee Press, 1983.

Guttman, Allen. *The Conservative Tradition in America*. New York: Oxford University Press, 1967.

Heyward, DuBose. *Mamba's Daughters*. Garden City, N.J.: Doubleday, Doran and Company, Inc., 1929.

————. "The Negro in the Low-Country." In *The Carolina Low-Country*, edited by Augustine T. Smythe et al. New York: Macmillan, 1931.

Hobsbawm, Eric. *The Age of Empire, 1875–1914*. New York: Vintage Books, 1989.

————. *The Age of Revolution, 1789–1848*. London: Weidenfeld & Nicholson, 1962.

Hoffman, Edwin. "The Genesis of the Modern Movement for Civil Rights in South Carolina." In *The Negro in Depression and War: Prelude to Revolution, 1930–1945*, edited by Bernard Sternsher. Chicago, Ill.: Quadrangle Books, 1969.

Hofstadter, Richard. *Social Darwinism in American Thought, 1860–1915*. Philadelphia: University of Pennsylvania Press, 1945.

Holt, Thomas. *Black Over White: Negro Political Leadership in South Carolina during Reconstruction*. Urbana and Chicago: University of Illinois Press, 1977.

Jarrell, Hampton M. *Wade Hampton and the Negro: The Road Not Taken*. Columbia: University of South Carolina Press, 1949.

Kantrowitz, Stephen. *Ben Tillman and the Reconstruction of White Supremacy*. Chapel Hill and London: University of North Carolina Press, 2000.

Key, V. O., Jr. *Southern Politics in State and Nation.* New York: Alfred A. Knopf, Inc., 1949.

Kirby, Jack Temple. *Darkness at the Dawning: Race and Reform in the Progressive South.* Philadelphia, Pa.: Lippincott, 1972.

Kirk, Russell. *The Conservative Mind: From Burke to Eliot.* 7th rev. ed. Washington, D.C.: Regnery Publishing Inc., 1994.

Kousser, J. Morgan. *The Shaping of Southern Politics: Suffrage Restriction and the Establishment of the One-Party System, 1880–1910.* New Haven and London: Yale University Press, 1974.

LaGuerre, J. G. *Enemies of Empire.* St. Augustine, Trinidad: The College Press, 1984.

Lears, T. J. Jackson. *No Place of Grace: Antimodernism and the Transformation of American Culture, 1880–1920.* New York: Pantheon, 1981.

Linehan, Peter. *History and Historians of Medieval Spain.* New York: Oxford University Press, 1993.

Link, Arthur. *The Papers of Woodrow Wilson.* 69 vols. Princeton, N.J.: Princeton University Press, 1974.

Link, William A. *The Paradox of Southern Progressivism, 1880–1930.* Chapel Hill: University of North Carolina Press, 1992.

Lumpkin, Katharine Du Pre. *The Making of a Southerner.* Athens: University of Georgia Press, 1981.

Lythe, S. G. E., and J. Butt. *An Economic History of Scotland, 1100–1939.* Glasgow and London: Blackie and Son, Limited, 1975.

Macaulay, Thomas Babington. *Miscellanies.* Vol. 1. Boston and New York: Houghton Mifflin and Co., 1900.

Malone, Dumas, ed. "Edward McCrady." In *Dictionary of American Biography.* Vol. 2. New York: Scribner's Sons, 1933.

Manent, Pierre. *An Intellectual History of Liberalism.* Princeton, N.J.: Princeton University Press, 1994.

Mannheim, Karl. "Conservative Thought." In *From Karl Mannheim,* edited by Kurt H. Wolff. New York: Oxford University Press, 1971.

May, Henry. *The End of American Innocence: A Study of the First Years of Our Own Time, 1912–1917.* New York: Columbia University Press, Morningside edition, 1992.

Mayer, Arno. *The Persistence of the Old Regime: Europe to the Great War.* New York: Pantheon Books, 1981.

McCurry, Stephanie. *Masters of Small Worlds: Yeoman Households, Gender Relations, and the Political Culture of the Antebellum South Carolina Low Country.* Oxford, London, and New York: Oxford University Press, 1995.

Meier, August. *Negro Thought in America, 1880–1915: Racial Ideologies in the Age of Booker T. Washington.* Ann Arbor: University of Michigan Press, 1963.

Newby, Idus A. *Anti-Negro Thought in America, 1900–1930.* Baton Rouge: Louisiana State University Press, 1965.

——————. *Black Carolinians: A History of Blacks in South Carolina from 1895 to 1968.* Columbia: University of South Carolina Press, 1973.

O'Brien, Michael. *The Idea of the American South, 1920–1941.* Baltimore and London: Johns Hopkins University Press, 1979.

——————, ed. *All Clever Men Who Make Their Way: Critical Discourse in the Old South.* Fayetteville: University of Arkansas Press, 1982.

O'Brien, Michael, and David Moltke-Hansen, eds. *Intellectual Life in Antebellum Charleston.* Knoxville: University of Tennessee Press, 1986.

Oliphant, Mary Simms, Alfred Taylor Odell, and T. C. Duncan Eaves, eds. *The Letters of William Gilmore Simms.* 6 vols. Columbia: University of South Carolina Press, [1953].

Pareto, Vilfredo. *The Mind and Society: A Treatise on General Sociology.* New York: Harcourt, Brace, and Company, Incorporated, 1935.

Pelikan, Jaroslav. *The Vindication of Tradition.* New Haven and London: Yale University Press, 1984.

Percy, William A. *Lanterns on the Levee: Recollections of a Planter's Son.* New York: A. A. Knopf, 1941.

Phillips, Ulrich B. Review of *Robert Y. Hayne and His Times,* by Theodore D. Jervey Jr. *American Historical Review* 15 (April 1910): 628.

Powers, Bernard E., Jr. "Community Evolution and Race Relations in Reconstruction Charleston." *South Carolina Historical Magazine* 95 (January 1994).

Pressly, Thomas J. *Americans Interpret Their Civil War.* New York: The Free Press, 1965.

Rice, John A. *I Came Out of the Eighteenth Century.* New York and London: Harper and Brothers, 1942.

Roark, James. *Masters without Slaves: Southern Planters in the Civil War and Reconstruction.* New York and London: W. W. Norton, 1977.

Robertson, Ben. *Red Hills and Cotton: An Upcountry Memory.* New York: A. A. Knopf, 1942.

Robson, J. M., ed. *John Stuart Mill: A Selection of His Works.* New York: St. Martin's Press, 1966.

Rogers, George, Jr. *Charleston in the Age of the Pinckneys.* 5th paperback ed. Columbia: University of South Carolina Press, 1995.

Rohrbach, Paul. *German World Policies.* Translated by Edmund von Mach. New York: Macmillan, 1915.

Rose, Willie Lee. *Rehearsal for Reconstruction: The Port Royal Experiment.* New York: Oxford University Press, 1965.

Rossiter, Clinton. *Conservatism in America.* 2nd ed. Cambridge and London: Harvard University Press, 1982.

Rubin, Louis D. *The Wary Fugitives: Four Poets and the South.* Baton Rouge: Louisiana State University Press, 1978.

Rufner, Reverend W. H. "The Co-Education of the White and Colored Races." *Our Living and Our Dead* (December 1874): 378–79.

Saville, Julie. *The Work of Reconstruction: From Slave to Wage Laborer in South Carolina, 1860–1870.* New York and Cambridge: Cambridge University Press, 1994.

Schorske, Carl. *Fin-de-Siecle Vienna.* New York: Alfred A. Knopf, 1980.

Simkins, Francis B. *Pitchfork Ben Tillman: South Carolinian.* Baton Rouge: Louisiana State University Press, 1944.

Simon, Bryant. "The Appeal of Cole Blease of South Carolina: Race, Class, and Sex in the New South." *Journal of Southern History* 62 (1996): 57–86.

————. *A Fabric of Defeat: The Politics of South Carolina Millhands, 1910–1948.* Chapel Hill and London: University of North Carolina Press, 1998.

Simpson, Lewis P. "The Southern Recovery of Memory and History." *The Sewanee Review* 45 (winter 1974): 1–32.

Singal, Daniel J. *The War Within: From Victorian to Modern Thought in the South, 1919–1945.* Chapel Hill: University of North Carolina Press, 1982.

Sinha, Manisha. *The Counterrevolution of Slavery: Politics and Ideology in Antebellum South Carolina.* Chapel Hill and London: University of North Carolina Press, 2000.

Sitkoff, Harvard. *A New Deal for Blacks: The Emergence of Civil Rights as a National Issue.* New York and Oxford: Oxford University Press, 1978.

Smith, John David. *Black Judas: William Hannibal Thomas and the American Negro.* Athens and London: University of Georgia Press, 2000.

Sproat, John G. *The 'Best Men': Liberal Reformers in the Gilded Age.* New York: Oxford University Press, 1968.

Stark, John D. *Damned Upcountryman: William Watts Ball, a Study in American Conservatism.* Durham, N.C.: Duke University Press, 1968.

Stern, Fritz. *The Politics of Cultural Despair: A Study in the Rise of the Germanic Ideology.* Berkeley, Los Angeles, and London: University of California Press, 1961.

Stone, Alfred Holt. *Studies in the American Race Problem.* New York: Doubleday, 1908.

Sullivan, Patricia. *Days of Hope: Race and Democracy in the New Deal Era.* Chapel Hill and London: University of North Carolina Press, 1996.

Tindall, George B. "The Campaign for Disfranchisement of Negroes in South Carolina." *Journal of Southern History* 15 (May 1949): 212–34.

——————. *The Emergence of the New South, 1913–1945.* Baton Rouge and London: Louisiana State University Press, 1967.

——————. *The Persistent Tradition in New South Politics.* Baton Rouge: Louisiana State University Press, 1975.

——————. *South Carolina Negroes, 1877–1900.* Columbia: University of South Carolina Press, 1952.

Tocqueville, Alexis de. *The Old Regime and the French Revolution.* New York: Harper and Brothers, 1856.

Twelve Southerners. *I'll Take My Stand: The South and the Agrarian Tradition.* 6th paperback ed. Baton Rouge: Louisiana State University Press, 1977.

Wakelyn, Jon. *The Politics of a Literary Man: William Gilmore Simms.* Westport, Conn.: Greenwood Press, 1973.

Wallace, David Duncan. *South Carolina: A Short History, 1520–1948.* Chapel Hill: University of North Carolina Press, 1951.

Walther, Eric. *The Fire-Eaters.* Baton Rouge and London: Louisiana State University Press, 1992.

Waskow, Arthur I. *From Race Riot to Sit-In, 1919 and the 1960s: A Study in the Connections between Conflict and Violence.* Garden City, N.Y.: Doubleday and Company, Inc., 1996.

Weaver, Richard. *The Southern Tradition at Bay: A History of Postbellum Thought.* Edited by George Core and M. E. Bradford. New Rochelle, N.Y.: Arlington House, 1968; reprint, Washington, D.C.: Regnery Gateway, 1989.

Weir, Robert. *Colonial South Carolina.* Millwood, N.Y.: KTO Press, 1983.

Weiss, Nancy. *Farewell to the Party of Lincoln: Black Politics in the Age of FDR.* Princeton, N.J.: Princeton University Press, 1983.

Williams, Raymond. *Culture and Society: 1780–1950.* New York: Columbia University Press, 1958.

Williamson, Joel. *After Slavery: The Negro in South Carolina during Reconstruction, 1865–1877.* Chapel Hill: University of North Carolina Press, 1965.

Wilson, Charles Reagan. *Baptized in Blood: The Religion of the Lost Cause, 1865–1920.* Athens: University of Georgia Press, 1980.

Wish, Harvey. *George Fitzhugh: Propagandist of the Old South.* Baton Rouge: Louisiana State University Press, 1943.

Woodward, C. Vann. *Origins of the New South, 1877–1913.* Baton Rouge: Louisiana State University Press, 1951.

Wyatt-Brown, Bertram. *Southern Honor: Behavior and Ethics in the Old South.* New York: Oxford University Press, 1986.

Yarbrough, Tinsley A. *A Passion for Justice: J. Waties Waring and Civil Rights.* New York and Oxford: Oxford University Press, 1987.

Zuczek, Richard. *State of Rebellion: Reconstruction in South Carolina.* Columbia: University of South Carolina Press, 1996.

INDEX